REPORT
2006

A MAN'S GUIDE TO WOMEN

REPORT
2006

A MAN'S GUIDE TO WOMEN

THE SECRET TRICKS AND EXPERT TECHNIQUES
EVERY GUY NEEDS TO GET THE SEX HE WANTS

RODALE

© 2006 by Rodale Inc.
Photographs © by Ondrea Barbe (xii, 140), Jonathan Storey/Getty Images (36),
PictureQuest (94), Anna Palma (166), Antoine Verglas (192)

Printed in the United States of America
Rodale Inc. makes every effort to use acid-free ⊗, recycled paper ♻.

Men's Health is a registered trademark of Rodale Inc.
Book design by Joanna Williams

ISBN-13 978-1-59486-359-2 hardcover
ISBN-10 1-59486-359-8 hardcover

2 4 6 8 10 9 7 5 3   hardcover

Visit us on the Web at www.menshealthbooks.com, or call us toll-free at
(800) 848-4735.

We inspire and enable people to improve their lives and the world around them
For more of our products visit **rodalestore.com** or call 800-848-4735

Sex and Values at Rodale

We believe that an active and healthy sex life, based on mutual consent and respect between partners, is an important component of physical and mental well-being. We also respect that sex is a private matter and that each person has a different opinion of what sexual practices or levels of discourse are appropriate. Rodale is committed to offering responsible, practical advice about sexual matters, supported by accredited professionals and legitimate scientific research. Our goal—for sex and all other topics—is to publish information that empowers people's lives.

Mention of specific companies, organizations, or authorities in this book does not imply endorsement by the author or publisher, nor does mention of specific companies, organizations, or authorities imply that they endorse this book, its author, or the publisher.

Internet addresses and telephone numbers given in this book were accurate at the time it went to press.

EDITOR: Deanna Portz

CONTRIBUTING WRITERS: Daniel Amen, MD; Mark Anders; Matt Bean; Nicole Beland; Brian Boyé; David Brill; Steve Calechman; Leigh Cole; Kate Dailey; Tanya DeRosier; Doug Donaldson; Kathryn Eisman; Christian Finn; Jessica Fischbein; Liesa Goins; Brian Good; Jim Gorman; Siski Green; Erin Hobday; Mikel Jollett; Ian Kerner, PhD; Colin McEnroe; Tom McGrath; Gordon McGuire; Myatt Murphy, Hugh O'Neill; Peter Post; Scott Quill; Phillip Rhodes; Lauren Russell; David Schipper; Lou Schuler; Heidi Skolnik, MS, CDN; Ian Smith, MD; Larry Smith; Ted Spiker; Michael Tennesen; Amy Jo Van Bodegraven; Greta Van Susteren; Mark Verstegen, MS; Sara Vigneri; Sara Wells; John R. White Jr. PharmD; Mike Zimmerman, David Zinczenko, Tom Zoellner

COVER DESIGNER: Anthony Serge

INTERIOR DESIGNER: Joanna Williams

PHOTO EDITOR: Darleen Malkames

PROJECT EDITOR: Lois Hazel

COPY EDITOR: Jennifer Bright Reich

LAYOUT DESIGNER: Faith Hague

PRODUCT SPECIALIST: Jodi Schaffer

Rodale Men's Health Group

SENIOR VICE PRESIDENT, EDITOR-IN-CHIEF *MEN'S HEALTH*: David Zinczenko

MEN'S HEALTH EXECUTIVE EDITOR: Zachary Schisgal

SENIOR MANAGING EDITOR: Chris Krogermeier

VICE PRESIDENT, ART AND DESIGN/BOOKS: Andy Carpenter

MANAGING ART DIRECTOR: Darlene Schneck

SENIOR VICE PRESIDENT, RODALE DIRECT: Gregg Michaelson

SENIOR DIRECTOR, PRODUCT MARKETING: Janine Slaughter

ASSOCIATE DIRECTOR-ONLINE: Matthew Neumaier

SENIOR MANAGER MULTIMEDIA PRODUCTION SERVICES: Robert V. Anderson Jr.

PAGE ASSEMBLY MANAGER: Patricia Brown

CONTENTS

Part 3: Two Worlds Collide

Part 4: Sex Matters

Part 5: In for the Long Haul

Must Reads

Part 6: In Check

INTRODUCTION

Every year there's an article that seems to cover all the bases when it comes to revealing the secrets to understanding women. This year was no exception. In the January issue of *Best Life*, Nicole Beland wrote one of the most comprehensive guides to understanding women at any age we've ever seen. By focusing in on the thoughts, wants, and needs—both in and out of bed—of twenty-, thirty-, forty-, and fifty-something women, she helps guys learn how to rock a woman's world with humor, interest, intellect, and paramount to all of this—sex. Beland also peppered the article with statistics about the male sexual animal in the corresponding age groups so you can see how you measure up to the guys around your same age. Take a look on page 19.

This year, *A Man's Guide to Women* covers all the bases with reliable advice and tips for catching a beautiful girl's eye, getting her number, how to play it cool, what to do when things get hot, and how to say good-bye when they're not. Believe it or not you've got the tools to get the women—and the sex—you want. Report 2006 is the ultimate user's guide for those tools.

In the over 250 pages that follow you'll find:
- **THE 30 HOTTEST THINGS YOU CAN SAY TO A NAKED WOMAN.** Whisper these in her ear and she won't be able to tear herself away from—or off of—you.
- **HOW TO READ HER LIKE A BOOK.** Why do so many women read romance novels? Is it really about the romance? Or, do we dare say, it's all about the sex?
- **SIX SUPER WAYS TO TURN HER ON.** They're a lot less obvious than you'd think.
- **HOW TO TELL IF YOU'RE TRYING TOO HARD, AND WHAT TO DO WHEN**

SHE IS. Strike the right balance, and she won't be able to keep her mind, or hands, off you.

   • **THE MAN'S GUIDE COST OF STAYING SINGLE.** A wedding may seem expensive, but your bachelorhood could run into money in other ways. Here's what a solo life can cost you.

   • **HOW TO PUT THE TIGER BACK IN YOUR WOOD.** Things go south sometimes. Here's nine hard-and-fast rules for awe-inspiring erections.

   Report 2006 has covered all the bases with the useful stuff you'll need to be sure you cover yours. Get started, man!

Courtney Conroy

—COURTNEY CONROY
EDITOR

The 30 Hottest Things You Can Say to a Naked Woman

COMPILED BY LISA JONES

1. "Good morning."

2. "Is it okay with you if I take this slow?"

3. "I can't stop touching you."

4. "Want to join me in the shower?"

5. **"I want to kiss/lick/touch every inch of you."**

6. "I love how you taste."

7. "Do you feel this, too?" ("This" being an incredible emotional euphoria.)

8. "Hungry? Stay right here—I'll make you a burrito."

9. Her name—her full name—followed by "wow."

10. **"I'll get the light."**

11. "I'll cancel my plans if you'll stay here with me for the rest of the weekend."

12. "No one's ever done *that* before."

13. "Can we do that again?"

14. "I love your [fill in body part here]."

15. **Nothing. Total, deliberate silence. You can stare at her, grab her, touch her, but don't make a sound. If she tries to talk, place a finger on her lips.**

GUY KNOWLEDGE

I f you've ever interviewed for a job, you know that the first step in preparing is to take stock of your skills, strengths, and weaknesses. To accurately represent yourself, you need a firm grasp on what it is that makes you who you are and how that sets you apart from the field of applicants. You need to be confident and self-assured.

Well, guess what? The same goes for attracting women! When you're comfortable in your own skin, you project confidence—and there's nothing more appealing to a woman than a guy with great confidence. Guys who know who they are and can acknowledge their strengths—and weaknesses—are the guys who get the girls.

In the following pages, you'll find everything "the guys who get the girls" know about women and themselves. Get ready to find out some juicy hints and useful knowledge for knowing yourself better and leaving the competition in the dust!

16. While looking out the window at people not currently in bed with her: "Suckers."

17. While looking at moonlight reflected on the ceiling: "What do you see?"

18. "I'll go make coffee."

19. "Waking up with you is even better than sleeping with you."

20. "Let's play hooky today."

21. Any use of the word "hot." Especially: "You're so hot."

22. "Squeeze my hand when it feels really amazing."

23. Words that end in "uck." Yes, even "duck," when appropriate.

24. "There's nothing else I'd rather be doing right now."

25. "I'm ready to go again."

26. "Damn, I've missed you."

27. "How about a massage?"

28. Playful laughter.

29. "Don't ever leave me."

30. "You sleep; I'll go check on the baby."

A Lifetime of Sex Appeal

In any room, there's one man who commands the most female attention. He personifies the physical, emotional, and intellectual qualities women desire. But what exactly are those qualities— and how can you develop and broadcast them yourself? A scientific investigation. Plus: The most beautiful and exotic women in the world reveal the traits they find irresistible

BY LISA JONES

THE MIDDLE EAST
SARAH SHAHI, 25
    TEXAS-BORN DESCENDANT OF IRANIAN SHAHS
    ACTRESS, *THE L WORD*

"Persian men are very lavish, and they're very ostentatious. I don't care who you are—any girl at some point wouldn't mind experiencing some of that. It's like, 'I give you a shoe made of gold . . . ' You're like, 'Okay.' But on the whole, what's attractive is when a man is open and not putting up any kind of facade, not playing the game. It's always the really simple things that get a girl's heart. You don't have to go out of your way; just pick up a pen and a little Post-it, and you're good. Looks are important, but it's not the first thing I notice. Maybe that's because of my background. I'm kind of a mutt: My dad's Persian, my mother is Spanish, and I was born in Texas. Growing up, all I wanted to be was white because all my friends had blonde hair and blue eyes. Then I came to LA and realized, *Oh, maybe it's good to be different.*"

SOUTH AMERICA
LEANOR VARELA, 32
SANTIAGO, CHILE
ACTRESS, *GILGAMESH*

"I think Latin men are much more romantic in the sense of serenades and the heatedness of it all. They love to do things to make a woman feel beautiful. American men do that too, just in a different way—a much more delicate way, I find. The things I look at most are the hands, the eyes, and the way a man treats his mother. It tells you how capable he is of loving and of giving and [shows] the quality of his soul. I find it terribly sexy when a man is devoted to his family and loves his sisters and brothers and is always there for them; that for me is very attractive. Sexy is not selfish, macho. What's also attractive is good taste—the capacity of a man to dress with style and with care even though it's a T-shirt and a pair of jeans. It's the quality of things and the way he's going to wear them. Because it shows an appreciation for beauty, and I think that's what women are: We're the beauty in your life."

NORTH AMERICA
GABRIELLE UNION, 32
OMAHA, NEBRASKA, USA
ACTRESS, *THE HONEYMOONERS*

"A lot of women say, 'I want a man who's ambitious,' and people take that as a negative. But if today you're a janitor, we want to know that you want to own the company one day—that you have ambition and passion and you're working toward a goal that's a little bit bigger. It doesn't have to be career related. If you're happy with your job, be ambitious about your relationships, be ambitious about a hobby or our home or about something. Have passion and ambition for something greater than yourself."

(continued on page 10)

Background

Convincing evidence suggests that it takes only one thing to get a woman's attention: money. (See Trump wedding, photos of.) But if you eliminate cash and gifts of Manolo Blahniks from the equation, it is unclear which of the more intangible attributes contribute to a man's sexiness.

Objective

To identify, quantify, and rank the traits that make a man "hot" to women.

Methods and Subjects

We surveyed more than 1,000 American women ages 21 to 54 in two online polls. One was conducted by Opinion Research Corporation, based in Princeton, New Jersey, and the other was done on BestLifeOnline.com. Both surveys took place in April 2005.

Results

We organized traits and characteristics according to the percentage of women who ranked them within the top 10 attributes. Women rated traits relating to character and personality much higher than they scored those reflecting physical attractiveness. For example, only 13 percent of women included muscular build as a requisite for hotness, while 66 percent placed moral integrity as a "make me quiver" characteristic.

Supporting Data

Top 5 Character Traits

1. Faithfulness: 84 percent More than 8 out of 10 women rated "faithful to me" in the top 10 attributes they find sexy in a man. A women's tendency toward attachment is a biological imperative, a matter of raising offspring right. Reassure her (often) that you're not going anywhere.

2. Dependability: 75 percent Three out of four women say they look for a man who makes commitments and follows through. Being responsible—even if it's just remembering to pick up salad dressing on your way over to her place—sends a positive signal that someday you might commit.

3. Kindness: 67 percent Young women may still fall for the bad-boy type, but more mature women are turned on by kindness, because kindness inspires confidence. In other words, if you treat the waitress well, your date figures you'll treat *her* well, too.

4. Moral integrity: 66 percent Having the guts to tell the truth means to a woman that you have the guts to be a good, caring, decent partner over the long haul. White lies are okay; just avoid any that are tinged with gray.

5. Fatherliness: 51 percent Being a good dad (or having the potential to become one) is about being a good role model—about being patient and caring, qualities women like in a partner. If you're not a father, then tell her about your favorite niece or nephew or the employee you're mentoring at work.

Top 5 Personal Traits

1. Sense of humor: 77 percent Being able to laugh at the stresses of this world is a must, according to the women on our panel. You get bonus points if you can make them laugh at—read, handle easily—the many difficulties that life throws at you.

2. Intelligence: 55 percent A worldly, interesting man is a man she likes to show off. Men who are take-charge problem solvers make women feel secure, and men who are always improving are never boring.

3. Passion: 46 percent Why have women always melted for musicians? Because rock stars are passionate in public. Women like displays of passion because they're not accustomed to seeing them from

(continued)

Background—*continued*

men. Get passionate about something: kayaking, impressionistic art, barbecuing, or Habitat for Humanity. It's proof that you care about something beyond yourself.

4. Confidence: 41 percent A man who feels secure in his own skin makes the woman in his life feel secure. By showing you can handle unfamiliar people or situations, you tell her that she need not fear, either.

5. Generosity: 38 percent This is more important to women over 35 than it is to those under that age. Generosity, however, doesn't just mean springing for dinner at a four-star—your willingness to give your time and lend your ear is what women crave.

Top 5 Practical Skills

1. Listening: 53 percent Pay attention. A woman feels safe and secure when she knows her man will down his BlackBerry and listen to her. Magic words: "I'm here. Tell me everything."

2. Romancing: 48 percent Romance appeals to a woman's right-brained, less logical side. Every woman fantasizes about being swept off her feet. Romance is bold because you're displaying your desire for a woman and revealing a softer, more vulnerable side that women find irresistible.

3. Being good in bed: 35 percent It's not just the orgasms. A woman knows that a man who takes care of her in bed will take care of her out of bed. (Of course, the orgasms don't hurt.) Your enthusiasm for her body is more important than your sexual prowess.

4. Cooking, cleaning, etc.: 23 percent Self-sufficiency means you're not going to expect her to be like your mother. Learn how to make one or two killer breakfasts or dinners, and you'll win her heart.

5. Earning potential: 21% percent One in five women surveyed said a man's successfulness in his career contributes to his sexiness. If you've demonstrated talent, goal achievement, and follow-through, you give women confidence that you will be a good provider.

Top 5 Physical Attributes

1. Sense of style: 30 percent The way you dress reflects on the woman you're with, and she knows it. The man who knows how to match a patterned shirt and tie will notice when she's dressed well, too. (And maybe he'll pay for the Blahniks.) Keep your tailor and your dry cleaner busy, and spring for posh, touchable fabrics like cashmere, suede, pima cotton, and brushed corduroy.

2. Handsome face: 26 percent The science of attraction, which has been studied ad infinitum, says it's all about symmetry. Imagine you have a dotted red line (*Nip/Tuck* style) vertically through the center of your face, down your nose. Are your features similar in form and arrangement on both sides of the line? Do your eyes and ears match up? The closer one side mirrors the other, the more attractive you are. Women in cross-cultural studies have also ranked men with broad chins, high cheekbones, and large eyes as the most attractive. Best way to improve your looks: Smile more, and make certain your sideburns are even.

3. Height: 15 percent Tall, dark, and handsome isn't the be-all and end-all. Women say they like feeling smaller than their men, but height doesn't necessarily mean might. They will feel comfortable as long as they aren't towering over you.

4. Muscular build: 13 percent Spend more time with the bathroom mirror and less time with the gym mirror. Nearly three times as many women value a clean-shaven face over the clean and jerk. Muscles help ward off rivals and assure a woman that you won't drop her during a dip, but your overall appearance is more important than the size of your biceps.

5. Fitness: 12 percent Women recognize a good body as indicative of a man of discipline and self-control. It tells a woman you can keep up with her, in bed and out.

THE FAR EAST
BAI LING, 34
SICHUAN PROVINCE, CHINA
ACTRESS, *MAN ABOUT TOWN*

"Asian men always try to be very, very gentlemanly, and they're interested in taking care of the woman. In a way, they make you feel secure because you know they're going to provide everything—it's in their tradition—for the woman and for the family. I think because women are more vulnerable—just in nature—we desire a man who can be responsible as a husband and a boyfriend and somehow give us protection and love in a gentlemanly way. In Asian culture, sexy is something more subtle, more subdued. It's flowers sent secretly or just remembering a birthday. It's not like a Western picture, filled with color, but, like a Chinese painting, something simple, with a lot of space left for you to imagine."

EUROPE
VAHINA GIOCANTE, 23
CORSICA, FRANCE
ACTRESS, *LILA SAYS*

"For me, the sexiest thing in a man is shyness. Spanish men, Italian men, European men in general are more macho, and I'm kind of against machismo. I've always thought men are more charming when they are able to show their failures; they're more touching. I think it's so sexy. I love the independent man—the one who doesn't miss you or doesn't need you, because I like to have my own freedom. I'm very instinctive; I'm like an animal, so I can feel if there's chemistry or not between our skins. It's like a magnet: You're attracted, and you don't really know how or why."

The Porn Identity

When does a harmless vice turn into a destructive addiction?

BY IAN SPIEGELMAN

I DISCOVERED SEX. I was 12. Great.

It was the mid-1980s, and I couldn't keep my hands off me. Then the AIDS movement, the Reagan administration, and Bill Cosby joined forces to keep me from getting my hands on any actual girls.

Conspiracy at the highest levels.

That was when Act Up—the AIDS education/provocation group—was doing its best to convince straight, middle-class kids that we'd catch a quick death if we didn't go in wearing chain mail. The conservatives countered that there was no such disease, but if there were, we should "just say no" to it. Prime-time TV, meanwhile, spread the Huxtable solution among my female classmates: Veil your budding young forms in such an ugly array of shapeless sweaters and ankle-length skirts that no one would ever suspect you of having genitals.

How could an honest kid sniff out a willing sex partner in a world so utterly full of contradiction? In the pages of a magazine, of course. And that's how I found solace in a sweet evil that would sustain and damage me for the next 20 years.

My teenage reality was drabness, lies, slogans, and fear, but pornography beckoned with a fantastic promise. *Leg Show, Penthouse, Oui*—what dreams! "Come up to the penthouse and I'll show you my legs," when the only things mounting were the number of strip malls and pantsuits. Sure, sure, sex mags were all make-believe. But they were honest and open in their way, easily beating out the dark deceptions society was throwing in my direction. Besides, those garter-belted goddesses who invited my gaze—and inspired my solo acts of devotion—harked back to a freer time I'd missed by just a few years.

But I did taste it, in a way. My whole idea of feminine availability had developed around a series of babysitters who supervised me on the cusp of my adolescence. They were shimmering party girls of the late '70s and early '80s who wore Daisy Dukes and platform sandals and saw nothing taboo in getting wasted or laid. Back then, being young meant Valerie Bertinelli in track shorts, Led Zeppelin, and a sack of Thai stick. By the time puberty actually took hold, I was stuck with Alyssa Milano in penny loafers, Huey Lewis and the "Hip to Be Square" News, and propaganda from the Heritage Foundation. But in my beloved skin mags, time was frozen: There was always that timeless beauty of a nude coed tickle fight.

There was a sort of beauty, too—albeit an acutely perverse one—in the very act of securing and using such heady stuff. I remember the adrenaline rush of walking into the smoke shop and looking into the face of the cute Indian woman behind the register as she gazed down at the cover of the magazine I was buying: two girls sucking each other's toes. It was wrong. Wonderfully, wonderfully wrong.

Perhaps best of all was the mad dash home, the forbidden literature stuffed down the back of my jeans, my heart beating in my ears. I dodged through the streets in a race to see what Sapphic misadventures my nameless girlfriends were up to this month. If I had to spend my youth with Benetton-clad puritans, I'd do it with a magazine across my lap, dreaming of a brighter future.

Of course, one's perception of reality is bound to be limited when "reality" is viewed mostly from the bathroom. While I was flipping pages, my more sociable friends were getting naked with each other at every opportunity. But I'd spent so much time along with my photographic fantasies that real, live girls scared the hell out of me.

By the time everyone was 15 or 16 and experimenting, I'd put in so many solo man-hours, burned my eyes on so many visions of the unreal, that normal play with another human being seemed unnatural. When I was 15, for instance, my very first girlfriend took off her bra for me. I put it back on her and told us both that I wasn't into breasts.

Things brightened in college, where no one even pretended to have any sense of prudence or decorum. Not only was there no need for shame, there was positively no time for it. In fact, I had such an easy go of it at school that I spent 7 years there, and I don't recall buying a single skin mag the whole time.

When I finally graduated, pornography hadn't played a part in my life in years. I was all set to be a grown-up, to have significant adult relationships. But there was a problem: By the early '90s, the happy hippie girls from college had warped into neurotic, metropolitan career engines who might let you get under their shirts and unhook their bras—if you signed a 15-paragraph monogamy contract and left a 20 percent deposit. How convenient, then, that right at home I had a machine that could instantly connect me to more debauchery than I'd ever imagined in my print-bound youth.

Joining a lesbian chat room on AOL under the guise of a slightly bratty 22-year-old submissive femme was surprisingly uncomplicated. And I found that I could maintain these conversations in one window while surfing for images to match the conversation in two or three others. It's good to know how to multitask on the Internet. But the big drawback of this strategy was that each of those windows represented a company that had my credit-card number, and I was being charged by the minute. Over the course of 2 years, I ended up owing roughly 10 grand.

Still, the cost was negligible compared with the price I paid in my mind. The Internet is Satan's superhighway. Go there with mild enthusiasm, and brain-searing come-ons follow faster than you can outrun them. There were times when the bizarre images had so inundated my imagination that a perfectly beautiful woman could be in my bed, and I'd think, *Why aren't there two of you?* I had plenty of relationships that might have developed if an easy alternative hadn't been at hand. Even now, as I sit here typing, I know this screen could be filled with women doing insane things, and I struggle not to turn to them.

I wouldn't go as far as to say I've reached a happy medium between fantasy and reality. I don't do happy, and I don't do medium. But my sex life is at least reasonable now. Put it this way: I don't look at porn even remotely as often as I used to, and when I do, there's usually someone looking at it with me.

The Unspoken Promise

Lingerie can be the answer to the riddle . . . something she hides
in the hope you will find it

BY JARDINE LIBAIRE

I KNEW HOW THEY WOULD FEEL before I ever wore them.
This is not to say I was born with taste. My youthful vision of my
adult future—in all its sexy, domestic glory—starred me in a black lace
teddy and leg warmers (this was 1983), sipping coffee from a mug,
waving as you pulled your white Corvette into the snowy driveway.

My ideas about lingerie and love have grown up, circled back,
been affected by the men I've known, the films I've seen, the dreams
I've dreamed—you name it. What a woman wears under her clothes
plays the same role as the thoughts she thinks but doesn't say: These
are blocks in the foundation of identity.

The connection between a woman and her lace is such an intu-
itive and intimate one that I am not always able to explain why I adore
the violet slip and hate the red camisole. I just know what I know. So
when a man bravely steps up to try his hand at finding something for
me, I am dearly grateful, unless he chooses a white vinyl nurse getup
with a red cross stenciled on each breast and a prop clipboard.

I should never say never. There could come some man, some
night, some mood, some hour, some place that might somehow make
me want to play Doctor's Office. Lingerie is a guessing game; its rules
morph according to who I am, who you are, who we are to each other,
who we want to become.

Of course, there are definite missteps to avoid. Give her a beige nylon-and-spandex bra and you might as well have given her a spatula or a bath mat. Control-top stockings send a message dangerously akin to a gift certificate for a teeth cleaning. A leather thong and matching leash should be presented to one who will appreciate the gesture.

If you're afraid the gift of a negligee alone says too loudly, "I want to watch you pole dance," you can pair it with something sweet, like Demeter's Angel Food candle, a bottle of Muscat, or Claus Porto's wildflower soap. Then you're announcing, "I want to spoil you rotten," even if you're still thinking, "I want to watch you pole dance."

Although a few gifts of lingerie can go wrong, an infinity of silky, drowsy, shimmering offerings can be just right. Great lingerie is a wink, its details able to footnote Grace Kelly's wedding dress, Elizabeth Taylor in *Butterfield* 8, geishas, the *Playboy* Bunnies of 1971, even simplicity itself.

Different pieces work in different moods. I saw a chartreuse slip with lace down the front, and I thought it was divine. But the distinction between stunning and tawdry can be as minimal as the flip of a fluorescent-light switch. On a perfect day, I hand wash that slip, hang it to dry over my Art Deco folding screen, and feel like the exemplary bohemian. On a bad day, I rip it off my body after looking in the mirror and seeing a Technicolor hooker.

Often women have a favorite. One friend has a hundred thongs in her drawer; another is a merry-widow connoisseur. I'm partial to seamed stockings, which have been an element of an elegant woman's life; ignoble commodities in wartime; and trashy, naughty playthings, too. When women in the 1940s couldn't afford these necessities of seduction, they drew the seams on their skin.

Some girls wear only sets of underthings. I prefer the mismatch. Under her charcoal-gray suit, a girl could wear Agent Provocateur, the glamorous, notorious punk stuff I spend my rent on. This is equivalent to the garters under a librarian's tweed skirt. A Dior Panther Thong under faded blue jeans is a pearl-handled derringer in the glove compartment. Under a summer cocktail dress, we wear tiny white cotton panties that don't quite cover everything, like the Coppertone baby's bikini bottoms.

Lingerie can be the answer to the riddle, a promise made in silence, something we hide in the hope you will find it.

The first time I bought myself something special to wear for someone special was freshman year in college. My girlfriends and I went shopping for Valentine's Day goodies. We sauntered around the shops, talking like old hands about intrigue and seduction. We had no idea what we were doing. I ended up with gaudy fishnets and garters and was giddy all night, holding my date's hand across the dinner table and skipping back to his dorm room. My own surprise for him was fuel for me. I thought we were the world's hottest lovers in his flannel-sheeted bed, his bong standing tall on his end table.

Sex with lingerie on can surpass sex completely undressed. As my friend Emily says, "A girl with high heels on and nothing else is more naked than a naked girl." When a man starts off the night by taking a good, slow moment to admire a woman lying in bed like an exotic butterfly in the negligee he gave her, it graces what comes next. And it's true, too, that style affects sex. The brutally elegant black slip with conical cups might lead to brutally elegant sex. Meanwhile, a pink baby-doll teddy, with its wide, permissive skirt and close-fitting top, makes everything sweet and dirty.

Men used to give whalebone for corsets to women they were courting. So far in my dating life, I have not received any whalebone. But I wouldn't turn down an appointment with Madame Cadolle, in Paris. The idea of having a man who loved me commission an haute-couture corset, the prospect of spending an afternoon in the room where Brigitte Bardot and Catherine Deneuve were fitted, this old-fashioned presentation by a man of a gift for me that would end in my presenting myself back to him—this would suit me fine.

Bespoke lingerie is by nature sincere in its tribute to one woman.

British artists Strumpet & Pink make wild and poetic pieces to order—Dirty Pearl panties are a froth of ruffles, while a crushed-up panty of black silk and sparkles is called Happy Days at the Courtesans' House. Jillian Sherry pieces are hand-painted, signed, and numbered. Like a kid drooling at a candy store, I fog up the shop window of Le Corset by Selima, in New York City, wondering who would sponsor a custom confection for me.

To be frank, the right man could give me a turquoise-and-black zebra-print nightie from the 99-cent store and I'd flip. Expense is not the point. The criterion is more basic. Lingerie should hang on a woman with the luxurious suspense of a stage curtain. A man should be able to slip his pinkie under one spaghetti strap, and the garment should slide in a whisper to her feet. The negligee should glow with body heat on the floor, and then it should be forgotten.

The Sex of Your Life

How to be sexy at any age . . . to women of every age

BY NICOLE BELAND

EVERY TIME I SEE ANDREW, the 44-year-old CFO of a small technology firm, he has a different but equally stunning woman on his arm. Sometimes she's a 28-year-old aspiring fashion designer. Sometimes she's a 40-year-old lawyer, or a 35-year-old divorcée who will never have to work again.

If you didn't know him, you might call him a playboy. But he's not like that. He isn't cheesy or shallow, and he doesn't get into relationships just for the sex. (Really. I know. I dated him—and fell hard for him—a few years ago. And as is the case with most of his other ex-girlfriends, we've remained friends.)

What makes women respond to him so instantly is simple: He strives to understand every woman he dates in every way, whether she's 10 years younger than he is or 5 years older. When a woman feels understood . . . well, let's just say it sweeps us off our feet.

So, for your benefit—and the benefit of the women in your life—I've written this cheat sheet, a concise guide to women of all ages—what makes us tick, what ticks us off, and what turns us on. Read it, and you'll significantly increase your success with the opposite sex, I promise. Just don't leave it open on your coffee table. If there's one thing women of all ages can't stand, it's generalizations about our gender . . . especially if they're true.

THE TWENTYSOMETHING WOMAN

WHAT SHE WANTS

Someplace new and exciting to go every Saturday night; a cool guy to accompany her.

WHAT'S SHE'S THINKING

The irony inherent in the gorgeous, vivacious, twentysomething woman is that everyone—single men of all ages, employers, advertisers—is eager to win her favor, and yet she's convinced it's the other way around. She's healthy and fit, yet so busy comparing herself with supermodels she doesn't give credit to her own smooth skin, taut thighs, or perfect breasts. She's ambitious and innovative, yet the view from the bottom of the ladder makes her anxious that she'll never afford a comfortable lifestyle. "A 25-year-old will have a nagging sense that she doesn't know who she is or what she wants, which leads to wonderful spontaneity but also compulsiveness and an inability to trust her own judgment," says Tina Tessina, PhD, a psychotherapist and author of *The Unofficial Guide to Dating Again*. The sum is a sexy, enthusiastic, charmingly humble, slightly spastic woman who is pure pleasure to date—unless keeping up with her split-second decisions gets too exhausting for you.

Another catch-22 of the twentysomething lady is that even though she often gives off a vixen vibe, she's fairly timid between the sheets. Her idea of experience is probably limited to the meat-and-potatoes stuff, and not the kinky fixin's. "I want someone who is a little aggressive and adventurous, nothing too hard-core," says Kate, a 23-year-old administrative assistant from Milwaukee. "Someone with whom I will feel safe and at ease, who won't put pressure on me to come quickly."

HOW TO GET HER ATTENTION

"The younger we are, the more shallow we tend to be," says Adele Testani, president and cofounder of Hurry Date, a New York–based speed-dating service that gives you a chance to meet 25 women in one night. "Older guys have to wear the right clothes and be in great shape." The right clothes, in this case, are sophisticated duds that are vigilantly in style—last year's leather jacket can add 5 years to your image. Eye-catching status symbols like a designer suit, watch, or car that men her age can't afford or don't prioritize also make a difference. "In my twenties, it was all about men with expensive lifestyles," says Samantha Slaven, a 33-year-old who owns a publicity company in Los Angeles. "Being taken out and treated to the finer things made me feel special. Now those things aren't as important to me." Invite her to dinner at the restaurant of the moment, an upscale event like a jazz concert, an art opening at an edgy gallery, or a black-tie party. And never seem overeager. The minute she thinks you want to be with her more than she wants to be with you, it's over.

WHAT TO TALK TO HER ABOUT

Her family and friends. "Young women love to tell stories about the people in their lives," says April Masini, author of *For Men Only: Date Out of Your League*. Make a point of remembering the names she mentions and then asking her questions about specific individuals. Recently released movies are another go-to topic, so make sure you've seen what the twentysomethings are seeing. If you know who Napoleon Dynamite is and which hot Mexican actor played Che in *The Motorcycle Diaries*, you're already ahead. If you don't, sign up for Netflix and get caught up. Never heard of Netflix? You officially have a lot of work to do.

HOW TO BLOW HER MIND IN BED

At this age, a woman is physically capable of responding sexually in every way, and she's probably having plenty of encounters. Yet because she may not know what kind of stimulation she needs to achieve orgasms during intercourse, they may not be very satisfying. Try the coital-alignment technique. It may sound like a surgical procedure, but it's actually a sex position that's been clinically proven to be highly climactic for women. (In a study in which couples adopted

INSTANT SEXPERT

The Male Sexual Animal (in His Twenties)

112: Number of sexual encounters per year
6.5: Sperm count, grams per day per gram of testicular tissue
<20: Minimum downtime between sessions, in minutes
71: Percentage willing to discuss sexual fantasies
8: Percentage who admit to cheating
15.2: Percentage with no sex partners in the past year

this position, 75 percent of the women had orgasms during intercourse.) Start in the missionary position with your weight on your elbows and knees and her knees slightly bent and raised. Slide your entire body up so that your pelvis is on top of hers, as opposed to between her legs. In this position, the base of your penis makes direct contact with her clitoris. When you thrust, be sure to maintain that contact. By moving her pelvis beneath you, she can help control the amount of friction, upping the chance that she'll hit her peak. Helping her have an orgasm will make her very into you.

THE THIRTYSOMETHING WOMAN

WHAT SHE WANTS

A close, committed relationship; dinner parties with friends; a skyrocketing career.

WHAT SHE'S THINKING

A woman in her thirties has all the ceaseless drive, feelings of invincibility, and itchy impatience that guys have in their twenties, plus the attention to detail and long-term planning skills that twentysomething men don't. She's starting to figure out what she wants—namely, the perfect job, house, marriage, and children. And though that kind of unflagging determination leads to great results, her reluctance to compromise is the source of unnecessary stress. "If you're looking for an inspirational woman who will support you tirelessly and help you achieve your goals, a thirtysomething woman will bring out the best in you, even as she demands the best from herself," says

Tessina. Highly sexual and willing to experiment, intellectually engaged, self-reflective, and ultimately satisfying to date, a thirtysomething girlfriend is the toughest challenge you'll ever love.

Also know, in the words of my 37-year-old friend, Amy, a dance
teacher in New York: "Women in their thirties are so horny!" Indeed
they are. Most any woman Amy's age would rather date a "cute" guy
who's as enthusiastic about her orgasm as he is about his own than a
man with model looks who finishes first and calls it quits. "Since my
body is rebelling against me no matter how often I work out, I'm not
going to kick a guy out of bed for not having a six-pack," says Natalie
Ray, a 32-year-old who works at an IT company in Houston. "But my
patience for selfish lovers is shot." Finally over the idea that good sex is
just for bad girls, the thirtysomething wants to get on top, make direct
requests, and experiment in new ways—which can intimidate younger
guys, who are insecure about performance and don't realize how damn
lucky they are. The more permissive and praising you are of her bold
and brazen attitude, the more fun she'll want to have with you.

HOW TO GET HER ATTENTION

At this stage, she is starting to see past the flash of superficial attraction and is more drawn to men who can help her achieve emotional and financial stability. "My ideal guy must be motivated
career-wise but also give ample attention to nurturing the relationship," says Ray. "He should be able to enjoy our time together and respect our time apart." The reality is that most men in their thirties are
so focused on getting ahead, they don't have the time or patience for
romance. That's where older, more-established men have a huge advantage. If you're passionate about your work but willing to make time
for candlelit dinners, late-night heart-to-hearts, and weekend get-
aways, let it be known to the thirtysomething woman you're interested in. When she sees that you can play the role of a go-getter and
generous romantic partner equally well, she'll be hard-pressed to pass
you up.

WHAT TO TALK TO HER ABOUT

Work. If you've just met a stunning 34-year-old, ask her how work is going, then follow up by asking if she imagines herself staying in that field or switching to something else down the line. "Women at this age are eager to talk about what they envision themselves doing in the next 5 or 10 years," says Tessina, "and they're equally eager to hear about your current projects and long-term goals." The only way you can strike out in this conversation is to not be involved in anything you're passionate about. To women in this hyperproductive phase, that pretty much means you're dead.

HOW TO BLOW HER MIND IN BED

With the knowledge and will to keep the orgasms coming like gangbusters, the thirtysomething woman is in her most sexually active time. Her biggest obstacles to pleasure are stress and pregnancy. Whether it's work that's preoccupying her or a postchildbirth I-don't-feel-sexy funk, it's going to take more than a make-out session to get her in the mood. First turn up the heat (literally) to make taking off her clothes more appealing and get her blood circulating. Then light a candle and kill the lights so that she won't feel self-conscious about her body. Lay her on the bed and begin to run your fingers slowly and lightly over her skin from head to toe, purposely avoiding her breasts and pubic area. Keep it up for a full 2 or 3 minutes before letting your fingers come closer and closer to her nipples and pubic mound every time they pass by. After 5 minutes, tickle, kiss, and lick her nipples directly. Then head south and do the same to her

---

INSTANT SEXPERT

The Male Sexual Animal (in His Thirties)

86: Number of sexual encounters per year

6: Sperm count: grams per day per gram of testicular tissue

20: Minimum downtime between sessions, in minutes

55: Percentage willing to discuss sexual fantasies

11: Percentage who admit to cheating

7.1: Percentage with no sex partners in the past year

clitoris and the surrounding area. Wait until she seems really hot and bothered before letting the serious lovemaking begin.

THE FORTYSOMETHING WOMAN

WHAT SHE WANTS

An honest connection that meets both your needs and hers; to live a fulfilling life; to be herself.

WHAT SHE'S THINKING

In her fifth decade, a single woman is still healthy, increasingly wealthy, and finally wise to the fact that nothing is perfect and life is short. "Fortysomething divorcées who want to remarry and never-married women who want children will approach dating far more openly and realistically than younger women," says Scott Benson, president of Debra Winkler Personal Search, an upscale matchmaking service in Southern California. "They realize that a successful partnership is the result of shared values, compromise, and cooperation." They're also more likely to have learned that it pays to be confident about their strengths, admit their weaknesses, and not take people for granted, all of which make relationships work infinitely better.

Some women at 40 are looking to have all the naughty fun they were too timid to go after earlier in life. "For many women, this is when our sexuality really blossoms," says Randi Gunther, PhD, clinical psychologist and marriage counselor in Los Angeles. "We're comfortable with our bodies and comfortable enough to let go of our inhibitions." Not likely to fake it, she won't let the action end until she's had her orgasm, and she'll call on years of experience to make sure that you have yours.

On the other side of the mattress are 40-year-olds who are more insecure now than they were 5 years ago. "For women who were used to getting admiring looks from men, the forties can come as quite a shock, because your age starts to catch up with you," says Gloria Brame, PhD, a sex therapist in Athens, Georgia, and author of *Come*

Hither: A Commonsense Guide to Kinky Sex. To encourage a woman who is self-conscious about her age, lavish her with sexual attention; reassure her that she still inspires lust in the hearts of men.

HOW TO GET HER ATTENTION

To attract women looking for a relationship, be humble and direct. "There's no bigger turnoff to me now than a man who still tries to impress with money, cars, clothes, or an arrogant attitude," says Theresa Delaney, 41, director of the National Confectioners Association, in Vienna, Virginia. "As for approach, the simplest words, like 'I saw you from across the room and wanted to say hello,' go a long way with me." Unlike younger women, who are turned off by overeagerness, the mature woman appreciates a man who knows what he wants and doesn't hesitate to admit it. She also thrives on compliments, but only if believable. "Don't bulls--t, because she'll see right through it," says Tessina. "Pick out one of her features that really is exceptional and tell her you find it beautiful." A woman who has worked her butt off in a career appreciates praise for her achievements as much as her attractiveness. And, of course, every mom loves hearing positive feedback about her kids. To attract the globe-trotting executive, be stylish and savvy. "Glamorous women want men who can fit in at five-star restaurants and *Fortune* 500 cocktail parties," says Benson.

WHAT TO TALK TO HER ABOUT

The hopes and concerns that are on her mind right now—whether they're family or business issues. "This is an exciting time for a single woman, because she's finally letting go of the life that she felt obligated to live and moving toward the one she's always wanted," says Bonnie Jacobson, PhD, a clinical psychologist and author of *The Shy Single.* Bypass the small talk and ask her what's going on in her life, what she wants, what's making her happy, what she wishes were different. Sincere, honest, meaningful conversations are what will turn her on the most. If you strive to understand her perspective—something younger guys seldom take the time to do—she'll be smitten.

HOW TO BLOW HER MIND IN BED

A natural lowering of estrogen levels at this stage in her life can bring on perimenopause, a precursor to menopause with symptoms that may include hot flashes, irregular periods, and vaginal dryness. But increased confidence in her body and fewer inhibitions about sex may make this decade the most sexually satisfying of all. First of all, make a water-based personal lubricant a regular part of your sexual encounters. Keep a bottle or tube of it in your bedside-table drawer. Now place a vibrator next to it. And a pair of handcuffs. And a blindfold. These hot little tools will keep things unpredictable and fun in the sack and help you avoid the pitfall of all long-term sexual relationships: boredom.

> **INSTANT SEXPERT**
>
> ## The Male Sexual Animal (in His Forties)
>
> **69:** Number of sexual encounters per year
> **5.5:** Sperm count, grams per day per gram of testicular tissue
> **1 hour:** Minimum downtime between sessions
> **49:** Percentage willing to discuss sexual fantasies
> **15:** Percentage who admit to cheating
> **7.2:** Percentage with no sex partners in the past year

THE FIFTYSOMETHING WOMAN

WHAT SHE WANTS

A loving friendship with little conflict and lots of space; to indulge in all the things she loves; to put herself first.

WHAT SHE'S THINKING

Contrary to what you might think, the kind of fiftysomething woman who is chatting up men in bars and restaurants and heading off on upscale singles vacations with her friends is anything but desperate to settle down. "Confident, outgoing, middle-aged women tend to approach sex and dating with a lighthearted, what-the-hell attitude," says Jacobson. "Yes, they'd love to share their life with a wonderful man, but they're also highly independent and able to make themselves happy."

And they know that the healthier and more attractive they are, the more marketable they'll be. "Many of the women I know who are in their fifties are in better shape than women who are 10 years younger, because they have the time and money to devote to taking care of their bodies," Gunther explains. "And the fact that they're living every day to the fullest, instead of worrying about the future, gives them a younger, more vital aura."

Quality is definitely more appealing than quantity at this point in a woman's life, and a deep, emotional connection in the bedroom is the ultimate goal. "Sex is still as important to me as it has been in the past," says Bernice Haberman, a 55-year-old teacher and guitarist from New York City. "The physical and spiritual aspects are equally important now. [What happens] outside of the bedroom determines how good or bad it is inside the bedroom." If a fiftysomething woman doesn't feel understood or appreciated, she isn't likely to want to get naked. The more you express how you feel about her and the relationship, the more randy she'll be. As for adding a spiritual element to sex, don't be intimidated—a little more eye contact and hand-holding will do the trick just fine.

HOW TO GET HER ATTENTION

Be out there on the dance floor, at the pool bar sipping a drink, in the audience at a concert, or behind a stove in a cooking class. "Active women want to be with equally active men," says Testani. "Women in their fifties often end up dating men who are in their late thirties or forties, because that's who they meet when they're out there doing interesting things or attending singles events." Once you're there, you won't have to vie for their attention. "Older women don't have any of the hang-ups about making the first move that women in their twenties and thirties do," says Benson. "They'll walk up to you and introduce themselves, and if you're not responsive, they don't take it personally." As for that shy woman in the corner, try politely asking her out for coffee.

WHAT TO TALK TO HER ABOUT

The things she loves: her favorite music, restaurants, movies, books, travel destinations—all of the potential things that you could enjoy together in the future. "As you move into the next half of your life, the simple pleasures seem anything but superficial," says Jacobson. "You really begin to appreciate them fully for the first time." Work and family are still important to her, but romance is the one part of her life that she still needs a man to fulfill. A return to the kind of dating conversations you would have had in your twenties is much more of a turn-on than talking career strategy.

HOW TO BLOW HER MIND IN BED

The onset of menopause can do a job on a woman's sex drive. Physically, she's still able to have sex, but psychologically, she may feel less feminine and desirable. The best sex move starts far, far away from your bed . . . on a tropical island. Take her on a vacation that will rekindle the romance in your relationship—romance that will make her feel young again. Take her dancing, kiss her in a Jacuzzi under the stars, feed her whipped cream and strawberries in bed. Let her know that she's still all woman to you. When you make love, try not to treat orgasm as the goal. Gaze into her eyes and just enjoy being emotionally and physically connected.

INSTANT SEXPERT

The Male Sexual Animal (in His Fifties)

58: Number of sexual encounters per year

4.5: Sperm count: grams per day per gram of testicular tissue

1 day +: Minimum downtime between sessions

37: Percentage willing to discuss sexual fantasies

21: Percentage who admit to cheating

10.5: Percentage with no sex partners in the past year

THE MAN'S GUIDE INTERVIEW

Billy Bob Thornton: "Take My Advice"

BILLY BOB THORNTON, 49, can give you pain (*Monster's Ball*), hit you with a whiskey-fueled gross-out (*Bad Santa*), then blindside you with inspirational heroism—as in *Friday Night Lights*, in which he plays a Texas football coach. When you hang out with him, it's clear that he didn't get the insight required to do all this from a book; the Arkansas native lives a balls-to-the-wall personal life filled with twists (at the time of this interview he was expecting his fifth child, this time with girlfriend Connie Angland), compulsive disorders (no antique furniture, please), and babes (Angelina Jolie, anyone?). Despite his famous quirks, Billy's bad-boy sensibility makes good sense. You see, Thornton gives a hoot.

On What Women Want

"Women don't want the sweetest guy in the world. For some reason, they like arrogance. Whether you're funny or smart, women like it if you're good at something—they love watching you change a tire. It's a fine balance: You have to show 'em your edge, but at the same time be sweet enough to listen to them, 'cause women want to be listened to. You have to be attentive and detached at the same time. It's tough."

On the Conundrum of Sex

"I can't live without sex; I'm like a full-on jungle animal. But I know too much about sex—way too much. See, relationships with human beings are extremely complicated by it. When you have a platonic relationship, you can say and do anything, but once the johnson comes into the picture, it's a whole different world—all of a sudden there's jealousy, envy, and fear. I think fear rules this world—and sex creates fear—so once you get involved in a sexual relationship, you can never *really* sleep again. When they're asleep, you're awake looking at them, thinking, *You're not fooling me.* So I've learned not to feel as much on a romantic level, to try to make the friendship the most important thing. 'Cause if you expect it to be like it was the first 3 weeks, you're screwed. The bond of the friendship has to become more important than the romantic bond, which drives you crazy."

On Marriage

"I think marriage is good—I've tried to do it, it didn't work out, and then I moved on. There's not crime in that. I've been married five times, and people think that's some bizarre f---ing thing, and yet I've got buddies who refuse to get married and screw 15 people a week. I'm like, which is better? At least I was trying."

On Fatherhood

"There's always a dead, absent, or mean father in almost every role I play, and I think it's my soul's way of working out [my issues with my dad]. Because I wanted to have a father. He was physically there, but I wish I'd been able to talk to him. He wanted me to be an athlete, which I was. I was, like, a star pitcher—but that wasn't enough for him, 'cause I wasn't a football player. It's like, Jesus, what do you want me to do? When you're a kid who was kinda mistreated or ignored, it can do one of two things: You either have to grow up to have children and follow in your father's footsteps and become a blazing asshole,

or you go the opposite way and overcompensate. That's the way I
went. I tell my kids I love them so often, they're like, 'Can we talk
about this later?' With kids, I don't care if they say, 'Oh, so-and-so's
dad is so cool,' because I'm glad they had fun over at his house. But
you wouldn't say to your wife, 'Oh, good, you're going over to see
Brad again. You guys have fun.' With kids it's perfect, total, uncondi-
tional love."

On Dealing with Demons

"I do chi kung, and the whole philosophy of it is not to clear your
mind but to let everything, no matter how horrible, come through you
and to think about it. Like, when my brother died [of a heart attack at
age 30, in 1988], people said, 'Go to grief counseling.' But I want to
hurt because of his loss. I owe it to him. I mean, say I'm married to
someone and I get run over by a train; I don't want her to marry some
other cat and not think about me anymore. I want her to f---ing
suffer. So I'm going to keep hurting for my brother. You want the core
of my philosophy? Even depression can be happiness. I live through
my depression and don't fight it, and, ultimately, I come back into a
lighter state of being."

On Growing Up

"My forties have been my best years. I'm getting more self-confident,
and that took a while. I try to associate with people who won't lie to
me, and I don't lie to them. And in the past few years, I've actually
become the honest person that I wanted to be. I'm getting way better,
I think, in almost every aspect."

QUICKIES

FERTILE GROUND

Check the calendar. Scientists have conclusive evidence that women tend to have more sex when they're most fertile. A new study in the journal *Human Reproduction* shows that the frequency of intercourse goes up 26 percent during the 6 most fertile days of her cycle—the day of ovulation and the 5 days beforehand. Women in the study submitted daily urine samples and kept a sex diary, giving scientific proof to a long-suspected theory. Fair warning: "A woman is more likely to take a chance during the times when she can conceive," says study author Allen Wilcox, MD, PhD, a senior investigator at the National Institute of Environmental Health Science. The spike occurs either because a woman's libido increases during fertility or because the man is reacting to her pheromones—hormonally controlled odors. It's also thought that sex itself may stimulate ovulation.

TAINTED LOVE

Forget the private eye—suspicious lovers can now use at-home infidelity tests to spy on their partners. The CheckMate Semen Detection kit (getcheckmate.com, $50) includes chemicals to drip on a suspect stain—say, on a bedsheet or a pair of underwear. A paper strip is applied, and if semen is detected, it turns purple within 15 seconds. Makers tell men to abstain from sex with the partner for 7 days before testing, to ensure that detected sperm is not the tester's own. If things are that bad, it shouldn't be a problem.

THE KEY TO HAPPINESS

News flash: The more sex you have, the happier you are, says a survey of 16,000 Americans by the National Bureau of Economic Research.

Economists David Blanchflower and Andrew Oswald studied links between income, sexual activity, and well-being. Their complicated scoring system and "econometric happiness equations" have one underlying answer: Get horizontal.

GENE GENIUS

Someday there may be a topical cream that cures genital warts. At least 50 percent of sexually active men and women will acquire human papillomavirus (HPV) at some point in their lives, according to the Centers for Disease Control and Prevention. Penn State University College of Medicine researchers have discovered a molecular therapy that shuts down HPV-induced warts, according to the journal *Gene Therapy*. A commercial product, which could also work on other kinds of HPV infections, is at least 5 years away, researchers say.

BREAKING UP

Could carrying a cell phone on your hip or in your pocket damage your sperm? Hungarian scientists have presented research showing that this fashion blunder may reduce sperm counts and decrease sperm mobility because of electromagnetic fields. Critics say the study didn't account for factors that might have skewed results and that more research is needed.

ASK THE GIRL
NEXT DOOR
The honest truth about women
from our lovely neighbor

The Thong Report
**What happened to thongs? It seems like they're less popular with
the ladies these days.** —NICK, ST. LOUIS

There will always be a core contingent of bare-cheeked babes who refuse
to suffer wedgies and visible panty lines. But for all other girls, the thong
was just another trend that came and went. They tried it while it was
hot, but now that women's magazines are praising prettier, more ladylike
panties, they're tossing their T-backed briefs and once again swathing
their butts in silk and lace. As with tube tops and short shorts, all you
can do is cross your fingers and hope they'll be back in style soon.

Let It All Hang Out
**When a woman says, "We should hang out sometime," does she
mean hang out or go out? And how do I know the difference?**

—GEOFF, DENVER, CO

Whether she suggests that you "hang out," "get together," or "do
something," it almost always means going out on a date, so I wouldn't
worry about telling the difference. You may think it's vague, but a lot
of women consider asking a man to hang out a pretty bold come-on.
We usually prefer to drop a hint that we want you to do the asking. For
example, we'll say something like, "I hear that new restaurant downtown is amazing. Have you gone yet? I'm dying to try it." Or, if we're
on a bus, in a bar, or at a party, we'll act fascinated by a man's relatively unremarkable cell phone, watch, drink, accent, or clothes, assuming he'll understand that it's him we find fascinating. Why be so
coy? Mainly because we want to avoid rejection, but it's also fun to
play cat and mouse, just for the heck of it.

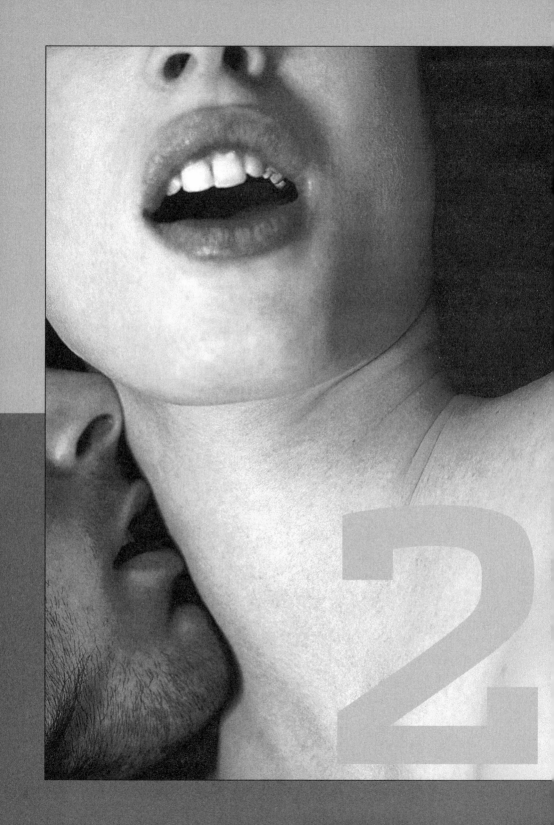

THE FEMALE MIND

One of man's great mysteries—the female mind: the ups, the downs, the ins, the outs. A few years ago, Mel Gibson starred in *What Women Want*. In the film, he was able to hear everything the women around him were thinking—quite an eye-opening experience for his normally cocky, somewhat-of-a-jerk-with-women character. He found out what the women at his job thought of him, how the objects of his affection were silently responding to his advances, and even what topics he should and should not broach with his teenage daughter.

Although it would be nice to know everything a woman was thinking so you could anticipate and carefully plan your actions, it's obviously impossible—not to mention the fact that it would take the mystery and excitement out of getting to know someone. What you *can* do, though, is read the essential information in the pages that follow, to find out what typically goes on in the wilds of a woman's mind. Want to know what women think about guys? What really turns her on? What her agenda is? What do women *really* want? Turn the page and find out!

THE GUY LIST

Nine Classic Observations on the Male Animal

BY DAVID ZINCZENKO

1. It's not the men in my life that count; it's the life in my men. —MAE WEST

2. All real men are gentle; without tenderness, a man is uninteresting. —MARLENE DIETRICH

3. Men should be the ones who succeed. It makes me feel comfortable if men are the ones who are in control. —ANGIE DICKENSON

4. Not only is it harder to be a man, it is also harder to become one. —ARIANNA HUFFINGTON

5. I like waking up feeling a new man. —JEAN HARLOW

6. I love waistlines that are not too big. I love legs, and I love hands, big beautiful hands. I like it all to be honest with you. —ANN CURRY

7. The only thing worse than a man you can't control is a man you can. —MARGO KAUFMAN

8. I think men who have a pierced ear are better prepared for marriage. They've experienced pain and bought jewelry. —RITA RUDNER

9. I have to say that men in general are a good thing. —JENNIFER ANISTON

Men We Can't Say No To

What makes a girl come back for more? Four women on the guys who make them go weak in the knees

THE BAD BOY

BY NICOLE BELAND

Here's my secret: I have a Tobey Maguire–Keith Richards complex. Most women do. In a nutshell: Good guys are boring, and bad boys aren't worth the trouble. My boyfriend, John, falls somewhere in the middle, and that's why he's hotter than any guy I've ever met.

Back when John was just my guitar teacher, he kept his strong opinions and sexual energy under wraps. All I saw was his patient, nurturing side. He absorbed my nervousness and embarrassment like a sponge and gave back gentle encouragement and soft-spoken instructions. He was obviously hot and talented, but his Tobey demeanor had convinced me that he was a shy loner. Not ideal, but enough to make me call him one day last August and ask him out for a beer.

Over six or seven dates, I discovered that this quiet, unassuming musician was harboring a lot of Keith. He'd dated exceptionally gorgeous, interesting women and had a huge cast of engaging friends, including a midget drummer and a guy named Scum who'd lived in his laundry room in the late '90s. John had performed at New York's most legendary rock clubs. In addition to being a sweetheart, it turned out that John was, and still is, a badass.

What makes this duality so sexy is that it allows him to play all the roles of an ideal boyfriend. He understands the line between spontaneity and unreliability, playfulness and childishness. He'll praise the finer points of Grand Theft Auto and a Bill Evans piano solo in a single breath. Man, that turns me on. He can also work knots out of my long hair, make delicious marinara sauce, call me on it when I'm being unreasonable, and talk about emotions without acting like he's doing me a favor.

But the sexiest thing about John: He doesn't spread himself too thin, do things halfway, or reveal his private self to just anyone. When he does decide to tackle a project or open up to someone, it's with high intensity and rare loyalty. One morning I watched him decorate a birthday cake for his 4-year-old niece. As he began to frost a #1 on Thomas the Tank Engine, I could tell that the rest of the world had faded away. When he's focused on me, I feel as if I'm getting 500 percent of his attention. He doesn't play games or hold back when he feels like grabbing me and carrying me to bed. His passion is directed carefully but expressed with abandon—it's so damn sexy I can't imagine ever getting enough.

THE QUIET GUY

BY SUSAN DOMINUS

The night I met him at a party, I wasn't sure what to make of the man who would become my husband. I noticed the bleached hair and the earring, which contrasted with a certain relaxed way he had of hanging back—it made me want to lean in close, to see what subterranean tremors and vibes I could discern and interpret. We were both runners, it turned out. When I left the party, I'd decided I wasn't interested. But I can think of no other reason than lingering thoughts of him to explain why the next day—a muggy freak of a scorcher in early May—I chose to go running in the park. I was only half aware that I was thinking about him when I actually noticed him coming toward me in the distance, a tiny pinprick of a daydream, first small, then emerging larger and larger, as if I'd summoned him from the shimmering asphalt.

The reality was better than the daydream: His shirt off, tucked into his shorts and drifting behind him, he came flying at me, all sweat, revealed muscle, and speed, as if that terse energy I detected at the party had been unleashed. I think I recognized him before he saw me, but I was too stunned and confused to stop. The night before, in my sheer black shirt and high boots, I'd thought I had the upper hand. Suddenly I was a shambling, unkempt jogger, running for my life in the hope that this swift-footed Adonis wouldn't notice my unglamorous transformation. Whether he did or didn't, he called me the next day, thank God.

I love his coiled energy, especially now that I've seen what happens when he lets it go. Some people love to watch their loved ones sleep; I love to watch mine run for the subway, when this ordinarily understated human being brazenly shows off a graceful athleticism that typically only I get to see, a secret privilege other women might not even know to envy. Some people find a quiet man unsettling; I find mine a pleasurable challenge.

He dissipates all my nervous energy, and that's a considerable amount. I love hearing him laugh out loud from the next room; I love the cut of his shoulders; I love the way he talks, choosing every word carefully. But even more than that, and I know this would surprise him, I still love the aura I sensed the night we met: a combination of mental focus, calm, and confident physicality. He makes my subconscious swoon.

THE WITTY ONE

BY SARAH HEPOLA

Back when my mom came of age, big-screen sex symbols were of a certain solitary, brooding variety: James Garner, Steve McQueen, Paul Newman. They were bruisers—mystery men who slung their virility around like a six-shooter. I never went for the type—too hairy.

My movie ideal is of another genre entirely—an '80s romantic comedy to their '60s western. Like millions of women my age (let's say

29), I find that no movie hero sends my heart thumping like John Cusack's character Lloyd Dobler in *Say Anything* does.

I know what you're thinking: *What a tool.* Granted, a guy shows up outside my window at 1 a.m., blaring Peter Gabriel, and I'm calling the cops. But I love a man who knows what he wants, especially if it happens to be me. Call me selfish, but I want to be assured of my importance, my irreplaceability in someone's heart. As a college student, I fell head over platform shoes for a chef who devoted an entire weekend to wooing me by cooking elaborate meals in an apartment we never left. I was impressed by his pesto, but he knocked me out with his gusto—he wanted me, he was determined, and it was intoxicating. I've heard from guys who swear that such behavior often backfires—women think it's too much, too creepy. In some cases, I suppose that's true. All I know is that the chef went after what he wanted, and he got it.

Back to Lloyd. He's not so handsome, really, and this is a key point: Charisma counts. His attractiveness comes from his quick wit and his generous smile. I can't tell you how often a girlfriend has described the object of her affection thusly: "He's not that good-looking, but there's just something about him." A swagger, an aura. My first boyfriend was the color of wood pulp and could practically fit in my pocket, but he had charisma to burn. He was hilarious and kind, and when he spoke, people turned to hear what he was saying. Because he wasn't conventionally handsome, I had always figured I was alone in my attraction, and it alternately frustrated and delighted me, like an amazing indie band only I knew about. When we broke up, women stampeded for his number.

THE MOUNTAIN MAN

BY MAJKA BURHARDT

I was trapped in a tent on a glacier for 2 weeks with a man I barely knew. We were in the mountains in Alaska, and an unexpected warm front melted the ice off the face we had come to climb and made travel impossible. Our tent was roughly the size of a twin bed, and as the sun beat down on us, we were forced to strip off layers until we were in only our underwear—and that lasted only until the first afternoon. For 14 days I watched the glacier soften and the man harden and didn't care that the climb was fast becoming a distant goal. By the time we went home, I was ready to follow that man anywhere. Maybe this would have happened with any combination of a man, a woman, and a very small space. But I think it had to do with this particular man. This particular man was a mountain man. I'd met him 2 months earlier in the Cascade Mountains in Washington State. I was taking a year off from college and looking for climbing partners—especially ones who had been out of college for more than a decade and had dark hair, chiseled triceps, and squint lines from too many days in the sun. I found just this man outside an Italian bakery in Bellingham. When he said he was looking for a partner, I said yes without hesitation.

He woke up every morning with a new perspective on each day, always concocting new adventures. When I was disappointed that we couldn't make that climb, he created a new thrill just for me: Wearing only his mountaineering boots, he'd stand outside the tent door and rub snow on his body until it melted into water running down his tanned skin. Then he'd crawl inside our little home and not let me touch him until I went outside and did the same.

We spent our first year together camping out of his '82 Saab. We've made love at 18,000 feet and at the bottom of the Grand Canyon. We've climbed together in Ecuador, Nepal, and Bolivia. After 8 years, he still takes the middle seat and always gives me the first shower.

Now we have a home above 8,000 feet on a granite hillside in Colorado. Five years of marriage and a place to hang our ice tools have changed us: These days, our outdoor pursuits are closer to home, and we use the foam mattress in our bedroom as often as our air mattress in a tent. Though I haven't seen a snow strip show in a while, other things keep me reaching for his hips: the way he waters our aspen trees and sweeps the deck; the way he hangs the hummingbird feeder outside 2 months before they visit—just in case. The way he does all of these things in an old pair of jeans and a too-short T-shirt that rises onto his hips as he works. And especially the way he acts surprised when I meet him outside with an ice cube in hand and remind him of the way we met.

Read Her Like a Book

Modern romance novels reveal the disturbing truth about
what turns women on. Heaving bosoms not included

BY JOE QUEENAN

ONE OF MY FEMALE FRIENDS maintains that you can't understand women without reading romance novels, just as you can't understand men without watching porn. Romance novels, she says, embody the hopes, dreams, and fantasies of many—though not all—women, just as porn embodies the hopes, dreams, and fantasies of many—though not all—men. (Right, all men; what was she thinking?) But then my friend told me that, in contemporary romantic fiction, oral sex and even a smidgen of good-natured lesbianism are increasingly common. It seems porn and romance novels are converging.

That got my attention.

So I signed up for the Put Your Heart in a Book Conference, sponsored by the New Jersey Romance Writers Organization. The gothic castle on the rain-swept moor in Scotland was booked that weekend, so they held it at a hotel in central New Jersey. Though the spiking popularity of oral sex in contemporary romance fiction was never far from my thoughts, I was most interested in finding out precisely what was going on in this enormous (400 women—and a few men—attended the gathering) but largely invisible sector of the literary cosmos. Ridiculed by serious fiction writers and shunned by critics, the romance-novel genre occupies a shadowy niche in American culture: ubiquitous but ignored, massively lucrative but sneered at, in part because it tends to encourage writing like, "The eerie call of a loon beckoned the morning sun." But it sells—to the tune of about $1.41 billion in 2003.

Until my friend opened my eyes to the potential for girl-on-girl action, I believed that most contemporary romance novels were bodice rippers with names like *My Heart Is in the Highlands; My Brain Could Be Just about Anywhere*. But by attending this fascinating get-together, I learned that traditional romantic fiction has been turned on its ear by "chick lit," in which the heroines are no longer sultry damsels waiting to be subjugated by stern taskmasters named Tristan d'Avignon. Now they're kick-ass, ball-busting babes who grab life by the throat. As a result, a convention that once offered such namby-pamby workshops as "From Once Upon a Time to Happily Ever After: Structural Guidelines for Building a Plot" now included panels entitled "Kick-Ass Heroines" and "A Day in the Life of a Profiler."

As you might expect, chick-lit writers are fun to hang out with. The heroines tend to be private investigators or intrepid scientists, and their creators like to talk about using peanut butter and jelly as a sensual unguent. They know the ins and outs of nipple clamps, the hazards of testicle fungus. And I didn't even know testicle fungus existed.

One writer, a spunky woman from the north of England, had just written a novel about an iconoclastic entrepreneur who launches an employment agency for out-of-work sex-industry employees. She also talked about buzzing sex toys and having once been detained at an Australian airport where the security personnel insisted on inspecting her carry-on vibrator. As well they should. But by my lights, *My Heart Is in the Highlands* is nowhere near as interesting as *My Hand Is Down My Panties*.

The single most interesting person I met at the convention was a native New Yorker named Alisa Kwitney, author of *The Dominant Blonde*. She freely confesses—with no velvet rope binding her wrists—that she read romance novels straight through her master of fine arts from Columbia University. Kwitney's books feature characters who escape into Walter Mitty–esque sexual fantasies or get mistaken for call girls while doing research for a psychology dissertation. You never find this kind of material in *The Wooing of Wilhelmina.*

Kwitney firmly believes that men can learn from romance novels. "If they would read these books, they'd be surprised at how little they know about women's sexuality and romantic fantasies," Kwitney explains. "Men tend to separate erotic writing from other genres, such as science fiction, mystery, and romantic comedy. Romance writers don't mind blurring those boundaries because we tend to see character, sex, and plot as all being mixed together."

In fact, there was no end to my ignorance of this important new genre. So that night I rushed out to a local bookstore, loaded up on contemporary romance novels, and conducted a quick crash course. It was quite an eye-opener. *1-900-Lover* showcases an out-of-work high-school teacher who starts her own phone-sex service and meets the man of her dreams in the process. *Hot August Nights* deals with a high-school principal who hires a baseball coach to nuzzle her mound and tease her pitching rubber with his tongue, though he inexplicably refuses to remove her panties, making her wild with desire to feel him against her naked skin. As is only to be expected. And *White Bikini Panties* explores a mousy young woman's abrupt decision to throw out her conventional panties and start wearing spicy thongs.

Honestly, I think a lot of male readers would have been just fine with the white bikini panties. But that's is not the point. The point is, in *Rolf and the Rueful Rhododendron*, you never get within a stone's throw of white bikini panties, much less crotch-nuzzling Don Zimmers.

Now, with all these dominant women around, you might think that I'd have been unwelcome at that conference. I certainly feared as much. Most of the women I know—and particularly most of the female writers—view men as a nuisance, a necessary evil. Not so among the lady novelists of New Jersey, who honestly seem to like men and believe that romance holds the key to happiness. Being in their buoyant company was a new experience for me: The very premise of the romance novel is that for every woman there exists a perfect mate, and most of the fun in life consists of finding that star-crossed lover— preferably one who removes her underwear after teasing her with his serpentlike tongue.

But here's where things got a bit worrying. As I was standing in line for coffee and brownies, I started talking to a woman about her burgeoning career. She was working on a book about a woman who opens a coffee shop on the New Jersey Turnpike and falls in love with the ghost of a man who used to live in the same building. Meanwhile, another woman was describing her novel about an intrepid archaeologist who falls in love with a dead pharaoh. I had wandered into the coven of paranormal chick lit. It included books about soccer-mom demon slayers who have to juggle career, family, and supernatural derring-do, as well as more conventional novels about women who decide to go back in time to track down their dream lovers.

That's not to say the lovers need to be human, mind you. *You Slay Me* concerns a female Keeper of the Gate of Hell who falls in love with a predatory dragon. Uh-oh. Then there's *Catching Midnight*, the story of a lovable orphan who is adopted by werewolves and fears that her new family will start sucking the blood out of Aimery Fitz Clare, her beloved falconer, because that's the sort of thing werewolves do. Then there's *Fantasy Lover*, the saga of a 2,000-year-old Macedonian warrior condemned by Aphrodite—or maybe it's Udonis Haslem—to service females through all eternity without getting so much as a back rub in return.

In paranormal chick lit, women are so dissatisfied with the merchandise available to them in the mortal world—Rotisserie League investment bankers named Jared Dyson and Navy SEALs named Cole Krieger—that they bed down with warlocks, werewolves, demons, dragons, moldy pharaohs, and 300-year-old redheaded vampires. It's not just that all the good men are taken; it's that all the good ones are dead—or, in extreme cases, even undead.

Here's another thing that worries me.

The chick-lit writers seem to be running out of chicks. It's not enough to be pining in a castle while wearing hot lingerie. Spunky private eyes, sassy bounty hunters, thonged profilers, and buns-of-forensic-steel psychologists are popping up all over the place, so chick-lit writers are desperate to identify some new professions to write about. At one of the panels, a writer who specializes in legal thrillers insisted that just about anyone—even a certified public accountant—can be transformed into a kick-ass romance heroine.

That's where I drew the line.

"My wife is a certified public accountant," I objected. "And with all due respect, I'd like to know how you could possibly turn a CPA into a kick-ass heroine."

"Well, maybe she's a CPA whose friend goes online and discovers a corporate scandal and gets murdered, and she has to solve the crime," she replied.

Maybe. Or maybe she's a CPA who used to be Napatha, Princess of the Nile, until Vyrnkk, a werewolf who used to be Julian of Macedon, seduces her. As long as it involves thongs and oral sex, I'm all for it.

But hold the testicle fungus, please.

Babes in Boyland

Women are charging out of college, determined to take on the world—with or without a guy at their side, even when the time comes to raise a family. Are men prepared to meet the challenge?

NICOLE BELAND

MY FRIEND ALLISON AND I are sunbathing on a topless beach in Mexico, and life could hardly be more perfect. All around us, bronzed bodies languish on the warm sand. Freddie, the resort's accommodating bartender, is walking toward us with two cold ones, a lime wedge lodged in the neck of each Sol Cerveza. I pluck an icy bottle from his hand and roll it over my flushed skin before bringing it to my mouth for a long sip. And suddenly I flash on Brooklyn and wonder what my boyfriend is doing at this very moment. It's hot, I'm buzzed, and I'm half naked. Do I wish John were here rubbing me down with SPF? Hell, yes.

Of course Alli and I desperately wanted our boyfriends to escape with us to this paradise. But they're stuck at home, short on cash—as usual. This happens a lot. Though we're hardly what you'd call fast-trackers (I'm a writer, and Alli's a grad student with a part-time job), we still outearn the men we love, who are talented and smart but, let's say, motivationally challenged, career development–wise.

We, on the other hand, like nearly all of our female friends, have been working nonstop since college, driven by three unchanging goals: (1) achieving a level of professional accomplishment that will lead to (2) financial independence, allowing us to (3) start a family by the time we're 35—whether or not there's a man around to share it with.

Not that we want to have it all without a partner, mind you. It's just that, along with being hopeless (if conflicted) romantics, we're realists. We've grown up with fewer roadblocks to achievement than any other generation of women in history, and we plan to take advantage of that situation. We understand all too well that self-reliance is the key to our long-term well-being. Like you guys, we're determined to control our destinies, and, much as we'd love to do it with you in more ways than one, we're getting on with our lives. Because the one thing we can't control is the clock ticking inside us when it comes to having kids.

I'm ambitious, yet I've always been laid back. I'm not the kind of girl who lives her life waiting for a man to give her a diamond ring. Yet I feel a palpable urgency every day. I want to live the good life. I want the keys in my hand. Most of all, I want a partner who's headed in the same direction. Yet here I am, on a beach at the Mexican seaside, and one thought keeps popping into my mind: My boyfriend should be here with me, and it's annoying that he's not.

John is 33 and everything I've been looking for in a man. We connect in all kinds of crucial ways. We can talk about anything and everything. Sexually, we're off the charts. But there's a glitch between us, and it's the same glitch I've felt with the last two guys I was in serious relationships with—the same glitch that Alli has with her boyfriend: We're speeding along life's highway, and our men aren't even on the ramp yet. They don't realize that the time is coming very quickly when women will surpass them in the cushy sectors of the job market—high-paying, creative, leadership positions—that they've always assumed were their birthright.

The latest national employment and consumer statistics underscore just how widespread this trend is. Women college graduates as a group start working sooner than their male colleagues do, according to the US Department of Education. Job status and security matter more to young women than to their male peers: Among women ages 21 to 29 surveyed by the Radcliffe Public Policy Center in 2000, 36 percent said that having a prestigious title is "very important" to them, compared with 27 percent of men in the same age group. Sixty-nine percent of those women rated job security as a "high" priority, compared with 56 percent of men.

A recent study by Oppenheimer Funds even reveals that women are smarter long-term investors than men are. We're more likely to stick to goal-based strategies and less likely to gamble on an unreliable tip, hoping to amass wealth quickly.

Unlike you, we've got about a decade and a half after college to get our acts together. While you're sowing your wild oats, listening to terrible music, and letting the dishes pile up in the sink, we've begun building careers and 401(k)s. We're buying cars, applying for mortgages, and generally behaving like grown-ups—independent grown-ups. We may be up for a tumble in the hay; we may even appreciate having a guy around who isn't quite as focused on the future as we are. But make no mistake: Our newly discovered sense of direction is having a profound effect not only on our gender but on yours as well. These days, it's not just on the beach in Mexico where you'll find us. We're likely to be the ones you're coming to for that interview for an entry-level, white-collar job we long ago moved up from. You may be taking orders from us at the office as well as in the bedroom.

Are you ready for this? I'm not so sure.

"Even if you're an enlightened guy who understands that it shouldn't matter whether your boss is a man or a woman, you can have negative gut reactions when the women around you are calling the shots all the time," says David Habbel, PhD, a professor of communication arts at Utica College who specializes in gender roles. "Expectations about the role you're supposed to play as a man are very deep-seated, and the culturally shaped desire to be in control is hard to suppress."

We're looking at a profound change in the way men and women

perceive each other as our places in the world continue to change. You can sit back and watch it happen. Or you can wake up, scouts, and be prepared.

NEW GIRL IN TOWN

The key to understanding today's young single woman is what I'll call the catch-35: the awareness in the back of every woman's mind that after 35, her chances of having problems with pregnancy or birth increase exponentially. The baby deadline is not new, of course; what is new is our recognition of the fact that we may have to underwrite the whole process, from conception through child rearing, on our own. In a 2001 nationwide survey of 1,003 men and women ages 21 to 29 by Rutgers University, 82 percent agreed that it's unwise for a woman to rely on marriage for financial security. That's a radically different attitude from that of the women of our parents' generation.

"We don't like to discuss it, but in a society where women are no longer raised to rely on men, women feel an enormous amount of pressure to make their mark before their mid-30s," says Lisa Johnson, cofounder of ReachWomen, a marketing consultancy that specializes in female consumers.

"Men face few penalties for postponing marriage," the Rutgers National Marriage Project asserts. "Unlike peer women over 30, they do not have to worry about a ticking biological clock. Nor do they have to obey a sociological 'clock.'"

The pressure on women begins in the classroom. And the prospect of being the main provider motivates us to exit the gates of higher education at full speed and not look back until we have a decent salary, a 401(k), and a mélange of vegetables grilling on the hardwood deck of a newly purchased condo. A husband would also be nice. We're not complaining. (Okay, some of us are.) But we're self-reliant to a fault. The staying power of our romantic relationships is not something we can control, and anything we can't control, we don't count on.

"I work hard because I never want to have to depend on a man financially," says Kori Shafer-Krzesicki, 26, a business consultant in Chicago. "You never know what the world will toss you. If I don't have to do it alone, that's wonderful, but I need to know that I can if I must. In a few years, I want to start a family, and I want to have enough money in the bank and my career on track to make that possible."

And, like 40 percent of young, single women in the Rutgers survey, Shafer-Krzesicki says that if she hasn't found the right man to marry by the time she's reached her mid-thirties, she plans to have a child on her own. "I'm not going to wait around," she insists, "with the idea that life doesn't begin until I get married."

All this isn't to say that we aren't focused on dating and marriage. On the contrary, finding love is probably the biggest goal of our lives. Eighty-two percent of the female high-school students interviewed by the Marriage Project for its 2002 report said that having a good marriage and family life is extremely important to them (and 72 percent of male high-school seniors agreed). But the terms of, well, engagement are changing dramatically.

"Years ago, women had to marry to get out of their parents' houses," notes David Popenoe, PhD, a professor of sociology at Rutgers and codirector of the Marriage Project. "Today, women don't need that financial security, and men don't expect them to need it—they want them to earn part of the family income. But by the time these women get into their thirties, they're in more of a rush, and they want to decide right away, in the early stages of dating, whether or not this guy is the one."

As Alli says, "Getting married is something we want to do, but it's not a feather in our cap the way it used to be.

"What happens," she wonders, "when neither men nor women

are working on making the serious romantic relationship happen? I don't know. I guess women are typically the relationship motivators. We still stop and think, *Wait, I have to get my love life in order.*"

MEN LIKE JOHN

When Alli and I returned from our Mexican idyll, I finally mustered the guts to ask John why he doesn't seem worried about money and job security, let alone marriage.

"Because I feel like I have plenty of time to deal with that stuff," he responded. In a way, he's right: Women's success in the workplace has taken a lot of the financial burden off the shoulders of men, who now have more options than ever.

Like 53 percent of 25- to 34-year-old single men, according to the Marriage Project, Jeff Jones, 28, wants a wife and kids—probably—but not anytime soon. "When my dad called me to say happy birthday this year, he said, 'Twenty-eight years ago, I was 28 and having my second kid,'" says Jones, who lives in New York City. "The realization that I'm nowhere near having kids or even getting married doesn't make me feel behind schedule. It makes me relieved that I'm not in that position."

The Rutgers survey also reports that men place schooling, full-time employment, and financial independence before marriage on their list of steps toward adulthood. Since many men now feel free to take longer than women do to achieve these goals, they're postponing marriage.

"It's only now that I'm starting to think I want to make a serious connection with a woman and take the steps that will lead toward settling down," admits Josh Bresette, 30, president of an advertising company in Portsmouth, New Hampshire. "Before, it was like I just wanted to do all the crazy stuff that you can do when you have no obligations.

"I think that's the difference between men and women," Bre-

Keeping Tabs on Mrs. Jones

I n college, at the office, and on the home front, women are pulling ahead of men in ever greater numbers, as these numbers reveal.

• **Girls Gone Academic:** In the decade from 1990 to 2000, female college enrollment increased by 14 percent, double the increase among men. As a result, in US colleges today, there are 56 women for every 44 men. Ten years from now, there will be 59 female graduates for every 41 male grads.

• **Advancing the Cause:** In graduate school, the increases have been even more dramatic: From 1990 to 2000, the number of male grad students grew 17 percent. The number of female grad students grew 56 percent. (Source for the above: National Center for Education Statistics)

• **Labor Daze:** Since 1970, the number of women in the workforce has more than doubled, from 31 million to 67 million.

• **Rasing the Bar:** Since 1979, earnings by female college graduates have increased more than 30 percent, while men's have risen just under 20 percent, on an inflation-adjusted basis. (Source for the above: US Department of Labor, Bureau of Labor Statistics)

• **Picky, Picky:** Among women with bachelor of arts degrees, only 32 percent would date someone regardless of educational background,

sette adds. "Guys have to get the insanity out of their systems. Women, I think, don't feel as if they have time for that crap. They get serious about work, life, everything sooner. I guess they have to because of the kids thing."

David Hirschman, 27, a newspaper reporter in New York City, says, "I didn't grow up with any pressure to climb the corporate ladder or gain a big title on my business card. I think my generation of guys feels less pressure to get ahead than previous generations did. We know our wives will have jobs and be able to contribute. I definitely while 59 percent of the men surveyed would do so. Once they get to graduate school, the women are even choosier: Only 24 percent said education didn't matter in picking a date, while 53 percent of men said the same. (Source: match.com)

• **Checks and Balances:** In 34 percent of married households today, women who work outside the home earn more than their husbands do. (Source: Bureau of Labor Statistics)

• **And Baby Made Two:** In 1970, 72 percent of female college grads had children by the time they were 30. Today the number is half that: 36 percent. (Source: *Mismatch*, by Andrew Hacker)

• **The Corner Office:** In 1995, just 8.7 percent of corporate officers were women; by 2002, that number had nearly doubled, to 15.7 percent. Nine years ago, there were 385 *Fortune* 500 companies with female officers; today, the number has risen to 429. (Source: Catalyst, a nonprofit research organization)

• **Home Alone:** In 2003, 21 percent of American home buyers were single women; 11 percent were single men. (Source: National Association of Realtors)

want a family. But just as women have a basic urge to get on with it, I think men have a basic urge to put it off."

Popenoe confirms this for the under-35 set: "The main reason for the delayed age in marriage is that more people are spending more years in higher education, and, especially among women, there are more career options before they settle into marriage.

"But when women think this way," he warns, "they wait too long, and by the time they're in their late twenties, they *do* want to get married. And then it's a little harder, and when they get into their thirties, it's much harder. Why? Because the men they're dating are also older, and they're looking for a younger woman."

GETTING IN SYNC

"The good news is that many of us now have the freedom to choose the life we want to live regardless of our sex," says Habbel. "The bad news is, by the age of 12, we develop very specific ideas of what it means to be male or female, and those expectations die hard, no matter how open-minded you are." In other words, our minds exist in the equal-opportunity world of *The Apprentice,* but our guts are still curled up on a beanbag chair, watching *The Brady Bunch.*

Most men want to date and marry financially independent women with careers that they're passionate about, according to the Marriage Project survey. Women, even when they're successful and don't need the support, still want men who can provide.

"Of course I still want the fairy tale," says Shafer-Krzesicki. "In my mind, that's to meet the man of my dreams and fall hopelessly in love, have two or three kids, and raise them in a good school district where the love of my life and I can watch their soccer games. That's my ideal, but I won't ever settle for a man I'm not totally in love with, because minus the man in that scenario, I can still have all of that by myself. It would be hard, but I could and would do it alone if I had to."

BRAVE NEW WORLD, AND WELCOME TO IT

You'd think the simple solution would be for young women to do what they've almost always done in situations like this: date up—go after guys in their late thirties and forties who have the same priorities. And some of us do, but that's not what most of us prefer.

"I connect with guys in their twenties," says Laura Trabb, a 24-year-old single woman in Austin, Texas. "We crack each other up, hang out the same way, and reference the same weird subcultures.

And there's no doubt that we're equals. I'm not sure I would feel that way with an older man."

Sure, I've had opportunities to date guys 10 years my senior who were buying houses, considering kids, and wishing they had a wife to come home to every night. But I couldn't help projecting a few decades into the future and imagining myself with someone whose body was sure to be deteriorating faster than mine because of both age and gender. Like Trabb, I don't want to be with someone who isn't into watching *The Big Lebowski* for the fourth time, or who has no idea that Johnny Cash and the Cure are cool all over again. And the prospect of ending up a widow for 20 years is no small deterrent.

So it's back to trying to get on the same page, or at least in the same chapter, as the guy I do feel connected to. We definitely have our awkward moments. Being with me has made him feel more pressure about his career. It's obvious that I have high expectations for him and for us. I think he appreciates that pressure almost as much as it annoys him. Now that women have the education, money, and willpower, there's no telling how we might reshape this world and find a way to flip that pesky catch-35 in our favor.

If Women Got Their Way

Our intrepid author cornered six women—and later, more than 1,000 of them—to ask what they would change about men. Their answers will shock the world

BY JOE QUEENAN

A **FEMALE FRIEND ONCE ASKED** what I thought was the key to a long and successful relationship. I told her it was to find a woman you could have the same three arguments with for the next 50 years, and marry her. I'm perfectly comfortable with the idea of spending my entire life having the same three arguments about money, sports, and why I'm so emotionally one-dimensional. But I would hate it if one day my wife suddenly started arguing with me about global warming, home decor, or why we don't have any Reba McEntire records. It would spoil everything.

My female friend retorted that my smug, self-centered philosophy was a perfect example of what's wrong with men: We're not open to constructive criticism from the opposite sex.

This got me thinking: If men were a brand and women had the opportunity to rebrand us, how would they go about it? Would they trash-can the current inventory and introduce a sleek new product line? Or would they merely tinker around with the existing model? To answer this question, *Men's Health* convened a focus group in which six young women, ranging from early twenties to mid-thirties, were invited to tell us exactly what is wrong with men.

The results were stupefying. Flying in the face of conventional wisdom, our panelists said they really, really liked men and, by and large, felt that their boyfriends, lovers, and husbands genuinely had their acts together. "I dated a lot, and I know what a great product is," said a recently engaged publicist. The great product was her fiancé, a gallant, debonair Brit. Added a recent college graduate who was clearly smitten with her beau, "I think the male population is pretty great." Particularly shocking was the opinion that men should feel free to watch sports to their hearts' content; one women even said she'd be suspicious of a man who didn't feel passionate about sports. The focus-group members also agreed that looks, while useful in stoking the first embers of romance, are certainly not a deal breaker.

"A sense of humor trumps looks," opined a panelist who had been married for several years. "If you're really funny and you look like George Costanza, we can let it slide. There are very few qualities that trump looks, but humor is one of them."

Money, it was agreed, is another. But money without a sense of humor is problematic. Particularly if you look like George Costanza.

Even when prodded to go negative on men, the panelists were diplomatic. Sensitive men were not highly thought of; as one panelist phrased it, "Sensitive and caring can quickly slip over into wimpiness." Guys who are too close to their mothers are a probem, as are men with creepy friends, men without ambition, men who pay too much attention to their physiques, and show-offs who condescendingly speak Spanish to the waiter. The women also had mixed feelings about Rotisserie League aficionados: "It's Dungeons & Dragons for baseball fans."

As for the women who went out of their way to portray all men as "bastards," one of the married women remarked, "Usually, women don't like men like themselves."

These opinions had me reeling, flabbergasted, stunned. If my findings were correct, the widely held theory that women settle down with an upgradable companion and then start surgically repairing his personality—with the wrecking ball of nagging—was substantiated nowhere.

If my data held water, I could immediately start work on a revolutionary book proving that men are not, in fact, from Mars and women are not, in fact, from Venus; but that both coexist and flourish on the very same planet, perhaps Uranus.

Still, I had my reservations. So I sought more data. *Men's Health* asked 1,376 of our friends at *Glamour* magazine to answer these three questions:

1. What would you like to change about men?
2. Do you realistically believe you'll be able to effect these changes?
3. Do you realistically believe you can ever change a man?

Here's where things turned ugly. Thirty percent of respondents to the first question came right out and said they deplore male communication skills. More than 16 percent singled out resistance to commitment as a major gender flaw. In the write-in section, the complaints were reasonably generic—smoking, drinking, talking with a mouth full of food, dishonesty, poor sex drive, spending too much time on the computer, obsession with video games, inability to get along with one's family—but some were not: laughable dancing skills and the inability to speak Spanish, whether used while conferring with waitstaff or not.

So how do we reconcile the two conflicting sets of data? Are you more likely to meet the pleasant, upbeat focus-group girls, or will your life be plagued by the Medusa-headed visitors to Glamour.com?

I'd argue that it'll all work out for you no matter which cohort you encounter. Frankly, I find it both shocking and reassuring that even among the *Glamour* girls, only 6 percent of those responding to the question "What would you like to change?" cited his obsession with sports. This clearly indicates that the young women of today are compassionate, understanding, and realistic. The only way to make most men stop obsessing about sports is to either slit their throats or give them lifetime passes to Los Angeles Clippers games.

More encouraging was the news that only 22 percent of the respondents honestly believed they could effect specific changes in a man, and only 16 percent thought there was any realistic chance of ever changing a man. But let us not draw the wrong conclusions from this disclosure! Don't consider it a license to start ogling women on the street or building even more solid, enduring relationships with even creepier friends. And it should not be seen as a green light to become even less communicative, even less chivalrous, or even more condescending when speaking Spanish to the waiter.

What it does mean is that whatever your faults—poor grooming habits, bad teeth, appalling dance moves, hair like George Costanza's—you need not worry that they'll be deal breakers. The women sampled in the online poll seemed to view men as a somewhat defective product in need of a repair job they probably weren't going to get; the women in the focus group thought men, despite minor faults, were just swell. Reviewing my overall methodology, I have now developed yet another theory: I suspect that the harshest criticisms of men in the online poll were probably registered by men masquerading as women.

Probably men who don't like sports.

Catch Her Eye

Every man in sight wants her attention. Want to stand out from the crowd? Here's what she wants to see

BY NICOLE BELAND

WHENEVER MY SINGLE FRIENDS get the urge to mingle, flirt, and maybe more, we hit the big, noisy bars, where we know we'll find dozens of men with an agenda similar to ours. But it's not that easy. We end up ordering cocktails and standing around, scanning a sea of suits. It's not that we're shy; we're just waiting to spot a cutie who we hope will be a little different—a little better—than the rest.

What are we looking for? Not what you might think. Yeah, good hair and an easy smile are eye-catching, but they're too common to pique our curiosity. Here's a list of the more rare characteristics that won't just turn our heads—they'll also get our butts moving across the room to say hello.

BEND FASHION TO YOUR WILL

THE STRATEGY: Demonstrate that you're a leader, not a lemming. Add an irreverent, original element to your outfit that hints (not screams) that you don't break the rules, you make them.

HOW TO PULL IT OFF: Keep 90 percent of your look appropriate to the occasion—you're fashionably astute, after all. Then throw on something ballsy. Suede New Balances with a designer suit (no tie) for an event at a swank lounge; a classic tweed jacket over a retro T-shirt for a dinner party; plaid wool pants with a hooded sweatshirt and Chuck T's for a concert.

WHAT SHE'LL THINK: You have the confidence to do things your way and the savvy to do them well. You're witty, hip, and a bit of a troublemaker. (That's hot.)

WHAT SHE'LL SAY: "Nice pants."

HANG WITH SLOBS

THE STRATEGY: Look appealing by surrounding yourself with your loudest, sloppiest friends—guys who emit female repellent. This can make you look, sound, and smell like Prince Charming. On this night, your goal is to attract women, not bond with the boys.

HOW TO PULL IT OFF: Sip while they chug, talk while they scream, smile sanely when they're laughing so hard Sam Adams is streaming out of their noses. And be the one to deal politely with the waitress and bartender.

WHAT SHE'LL THINK: You're not swayed by peer pressure, and you're in control enough to be a gentleman on a boys' night out. Plus, her maternal instincts will kick in, making her want to rescue you from those animals.

WHAT SHE'LL SAY: "Always so well behaved?"

READ, WATCH, LISTEN

THE STRATEGY: Know something about everything, so you'll have something to talk about. Party talk ping-pongs between politics, film, music, and celebrities, so the more you've seen, heard, and read, the more seductive your banter will be. It takes just one hit—"I love Fountains of Wayne!"—and she'll want to spend more time with you.

HOW TO PULL IT OFF: It's not often that a man who reads *The Economist* and owns a Fellini box set ends up with a girl at each elbow. We like a guy who's seen last night's *Daily Show*, reads *Radar*, and knows which blogs deliver the best dirt. Do a quick late-breaking-news-and-gossip check before heading out for the night, and then drop what you know when a beautiful woman can overhear it. (And it's okay to read *The Economist*; that strategy works wonders with educated Euro babes.)

WHAT SHE'LL THINK: Finally, here's a guy who can tell her something she doesn't already know, something she'll want to repeat to her friends in the morning.

WHAT SHE'LL SAY: "I'm sorry, did you just say that Katie is having Tom's baby?"

BARELY NOTICE THE ÜBERBABE

THE STRATEGY: Remain blasé when a decked-out bombshell strolls by and you'll send the message that you're too smart to be wowed by a Wonderbra and red lipstick.

HOW TO PULL IT OFF: We don't blame you for looking. But it makes us cringe when one male head after another swivels in her direction. What we love to see is a man who raises his eyes to see what the commotion is about, nonchalantly registers the hottie, then doesn't seem to give her another thought.

WHAT SHE'LL THINK: You've had too much experience with high-maintenance women to become excited by yet another would-be model. Or, even better, you prefer women who look as if they have more interesting things to do than primp in front of a mirror.

WHAT SHE'LL SAY: "I hope you're not gay."

GO DEEP

THE STRATEGY: Appear thoughtful by focusing intently on something unobtrusive.

HOW TO PULL IT OFF: Wander away from the crowd, take in the scene, then find a painting, book, view out a window, whatever—not the jukebox—and pore over the details. You're oblivious to the commotion.

WHAT SHE'LL THINK: You're sensitive and smart and, if you furrow your brow, intense. Women love intense. It's very mysterious, very sexy, very Benicio Del Toro. She'll want to plumb the depths of your brooding mind.

WHAT SHE'LL SAY: "What's so fascinating?"

GIVE SOMEONE A HAND

THE STRATEGY: Loud, crowded places foster an "every man for himself" attitude. To rise above it, go out of your way to be helpful.

HOW TO PULL IT OFF: Help a girl who's trying to reach over people to get her drink from the bartender. Give your place in the unisex bathroom line to an anxious-looking woman.

WHAT SHE'LL THINK: You're so thoughtful . . . Could such a great guy still be single?

WHAT SHE'LL SAY: "So chivalry isn't dead."

GET SOME AIR

THE STRATEGY: Establish a thoughtful-loner vibe, and facilitate conversation.

HOW TO PULL IT OFF: Stepping out for a cell call or smoke is off-putting, not alluring. Going out for some air is romantic. Make like Bogart, sans cigarette, and lean against the wall, hands in your pockets, gazing into the middle distance. If a conversation starts, great. If not, women will notice you as an individual before you rejoin the faceless mob.

WHAT SHE'LL THINK: We're out here; everyone else is in there. Maybe it was meant to be.

WHAT SHE'LL SAY: "Hey there."

5 Things You Should Never Say to a Woman

Interested in a life of constant arguing, withering stares, and no sex?
Just keep using these phrases

BY SARAH MILLER

WOMEN FREAK OUT. Often at you. Often for no discernible reason.

You say something that you consider totally innocuous or even downright nice, only to find that you've offended, enraged, or annoyed us.

Your first problem—being attracted to women, a very weird group of people—is not going to go away. But here's a problem you can solve: word choice. You need to know the phrases that, once introduced to her volatile atmosphere, will result in explosion (or quiet contempt—no picnic, either). Then you need to strike them from your vocabulary.

Warning: Some of these absolute no-no words and phrases seem so incredibly harmless, you may think we're kidding. We're not.

FORBIDDEN PHRASE #1: "RELAX"

It might seem logical to you to tell a woman who's freaking out to relax. And if "logical" meant the same thing as "stupidest idea ever," you'd be correct. Understand, a woman screaming and carrying on in anger or frustration or panic thinks that her response is 100 percent appropriate. If the inciting situation has anything to do with you, she feels she has a responsibility to freak out extra to compensate for your maddening calm.

So when you tell her to relax, you're implying that your response—i.e., nothing—is correct. You're denying that there's a reason to be upset. You're telling her she's crazy. Women may sometimes feel crazy and joke about it, but anything smacking of accusations of being crazy will be far from soothing.

SAY . . . "I'm just as upset about this as you are. Let's deal with it together." This way she knows you're totally sympathetic. This should help her to . . . oh, God . . . relax.

FORBIDDEN PHRASE #2: "I LOVE YOU" (DURING A FIGHT)

In movies, "I love you" is usually employed by men during I-love-you-appropriate situations—lovemaking, walks on the beach, airport reunions. In real life, a woman hears "I love you" most often at that point in a fight when she desperately wants to get to the heart of the issue, and when you desperately want to stop this nonsense and watch *Alias*—which you normally don't even watch.

When you come home shirtless from a bachelor party or forget our birthdays and stand there in the face of our rage and crushing disappointment, do you really believe that merely stating the powerful existence of your love is going to make everything okay? Because it's not.

SAY . . .

1. "[Insert detailed explanation of what you did and why you did it.]"
2. "It won't happen again."
3. "I love you." (It's okay at the end of the apology, just not at the beginning.)

And when you go to a bachelor party, take along an extra shirt.

FORBIDDEN PHRASE #3: "IT'S UP TO YOU" (AKA "WHATEVER YOU WANT TO DO IS FINE WITH ME")

Relationships are full of decisions. You decide where to eat, where to go on vacation, where to send your child to preschool. Most men wouldn't dream of looking at their wife or girlfriend and saying, "You know what? I just don't care." They would, however, say, "It's up to you." And find themselves in a world of hurt they never saw coming.

Men think of decision making as work without pay. For women, it's like window-shopping for life's possibilities, and we want you to help us shop. So when you say, "It's up to you," we feel abandoned.

SAY . . . "I could definitely do A or B, but I'm not crazy about C. What are you thinking?" This shows you're listening, suggests you care, and gets you out of deciding.

FORBIDDEN PHRASE #4: "YOU KNEW I WAS THIS WAY WHEN YOU MARRIED ME"

Well, the truth is that we didn't. Or we knew deep down, but we were so busy enjoying our fantasy of you that we chose to ignore what was really there. It's not your fault. It's just that when we were little, we spent so much time daydreaming about having the perfect life. Now that we're actually in grown-up life, we can't turn off our daydreaming switch. Telling a woman "You knew I was this way when you married me" is like saying the way your life is right now is the way it's going to be forever and ever. And that may well be true—in many wonderful and not-so-wonderful ways. But if she were to accept that, a little part of her would die.

SAY . . . "It frustrates me, too—and I'm working on it." It's a lie. That's okay.

FORBIDDEN PHRASE #5: (NOTHING)

At times, you may be afraid of saying the wrong thing. You may think, *If I just keep my mouth shut, I'll be okay.* Well, no. Imagine you're pitching in a baseball game in which there is no hitter, not even a catcher. You would not enjoy that. Imagine yourself, head hanging, going to retrieve the ball yourself and, once again, throwing it to no one. That's how we feel when you don't talk to us.

SAY . . . Anything. Throw the ball back. Throw it badly. Even risk throwing a wild pitch and letting her take an extra base. But keep your head in the game.

What Her Body Is Telling You

10 subtle signs of what she's thinking and feeling

BY DAVID SCHIPPER AND LISA JONES

PUPILS

If she's feeling stimulated by you (not just sexually), her pupils will dilate. That's because her body is programmed to want to see more of whatever's exciting her, so her brain tells her irises to let in more light. Bonus: As the inkiness spreads, she'll start looking better to you, too. Research shows that men rate women with larger pupils as more attractive. Time to make your move.

EYELASHES

Hold her gaze for a minute. If she's blinking more than normal (which is about 15 times a minute), there's a good chance she's on the Pill; women on birth control blink 32 percent more than those who aren't. Aside from the obvious, what does that mean for you? Put on your toughest, most confident mug as you look at her. Because of the shift in hormone levels, research says, women on the Pill are more attracted to men with rugged features, such as strong, wide jaws.

BRAIN

She's matching you drink for drink; you're starting to feel like re-enacting *Animal House*, but she seems like her same old self. What's the deal? Men and women get different kinds of buzzes: Men lose inhibitions, while women become sedated. If you're looking to get her into the party spirit, don't feed her more alcohol. Instead, feed the jukebox. Research shows that mid- to fast-tempo music will make her more social.

BELLY

Want to know if it's a good or bad time to broach a tricky conversation? You can tell if she's suitably relaxed by her breathing pattern. If her stomach pulls in with each inhalation, she's taking shallow breaths from her chest, which indicates stress. Keep your distance. If her abdomen and chest expand with each inhalation, she's taking deeper, more rhythmic breaths—a sign of relaxation. Go for it.

NOSE

Her sense of smell is sharpest first thing in the morning, which, aside from being a good reason to brush your teeth immediately, makes it the best time to impress her with your culinary skills. That's because 90 percent of taste is really smell. Treat her to a breakfast in bed consisting of warmed banana-nut bread, which has an aroma that, according to one study, increases bloodflow to the vagina. And that may lead to a different kind of morning treat.

CHEST

Sex flush, a pinkish look to the skin of her chest, occurs during foreplay. It stems from changes in blood pressure and circulation, along with pulse and respiration rates. Think of it as her coy way of telling you that if you keep doing what you're doing, you just might get lucky. Another sign that things are working: A woman's breasts grow by as much as 25 percent as things turn hot and heavy.

SMALL OF HER BACK

As she moves toward orgasm during sex, she'll begin to arch her back. Hold her tight around the small of her back at this point and stay attuned to how much she's arching. And, for God's sake, do not let up; maintain the same rhythm and intensity of stimulation until she climaxes. She'll pay you back for this later, with interest.

FINGERNAILS

Pay attention to her fingers; among the surest signs of anxiety or de-pression in a woman are body-focused repetitive behaviors, such as skin picking and nail biting. If you see her doing that, don't nag her to stop; that can send her deeper into a spiral. Instead, gently pull her hand away, give it a squeeze, and hold on to it. Feel the tension ooze right out.

HANDS

If it seems as if she always has cold hands, that's because she does—almost 3 degrees colder than yours, possibly more if she's stressed. Women's bodies, even more than men's, are programmed to keep their cores warmer than their extremities. So to warm her hands up, don't massage them; wrap your arm around her waist. This will warm her core and allow blood to flow back into her hands.

BETWEEN HER LEGS

Okay, you know enough about your partner's menstrual cycle to know when to leave her alone. Now add this to your arsenal: Two weeks after her period begins, she will be at her horniest, guaranteed. Fe-male sexual motivation is highest when she's ovulating. Warning: This is also when she's most likely to get pregnant.

Monogamy Rules

A few things to remember before you cheat on a woman
BY MIKE ZIMMERMAN

1. When presented with the ideal cheating scenario—that is, if a flying saucer lands in the cornfield where you happen to be standing and a female alien of sinus-clearing hotness slithers down the ramp and declares that she wants to come in peace a minimum of four times in the next hour, and you take her up on it because you know no one will ever find out—no one must ever find out.

2. Someone will always find out.

3. If you get caught, the law is on your wife's side. And you won't lose just half of your stuff. The other half—the golf clubs, the surround sound, the Armani—will be destroyed in a spectacular driveway bonfire as every angry woman you know toasts marshmallows shaped like your testicles.

4. And if you're not married? Your longtime girl is bound by no law.

5. Yes, traveling for business is lonely. Phone home for a bi-coastal quickie.

6. Or, to paraphrase Neil Simon, do to yourself what you would otherwise do unto others.

7. If a woman who knows you're spoken for comes on to you, it's flattering. It's tempting. But remember that she's doing it to feed her own ego, not yours. She wants to see how much power she holds over you. And if you take her bait, she then knows she must be superior in every way to your sweetie. Deep down, she has nothing but contempt for both your male weakness and your mate's existence. That should really piss you off.

8. According to the Shari'ah, the laws of ancient Islam, adulterers must be stoned to death. Before you say, "Dude, cool," we mean with rocks. In these parts, that's what will happen to your good name. Friends you made while you were a couple will disappear. Friends you had as a single guy are long gone. That leaves you with the hard drinkers.

9. You're about to be with the kind of woman who wants to be with the kind of man who would cheat on a woman.

10. Channel all temptation toward the girl you left at home. Example: When out for a night with the boys, go to Hooters, not a strip club or roadhouse. Hooters girls are the unsung heroines of relationship therapy—gorgeous, chatty, and so untouchable that you always go home hungry. Your gal has no idea her sex life will improve tenfold when you get there.

11. At the office party, pretend the coworker who's flirting with you has gonorrhea.

12. "I'm famous for all the wrong reasons."—Joey Buttafuoco

13. If your ex calls, enjoy a pleasant 5-minute conversation. Then tell her your wife's on the other line.

14. Treat your temptation as a cage match. Defeating that treacherous organ between your legs is the ultimate triumph of man over nature. It's you versus your penis. He's up for the challenge. Are you?

Unforgettable

Five women reveal the secrets of their hottest hookups ever.
Read and revel

Anonymous Sex

He was my fantasy guy. I got the hotel room

By Mara Levy

Every woman holds an image in her mental wallet of what her perfect lover looks like, and she's spent more than a little alone time playing out a chance meeting with him in her head. Two years ago, I found my fantasy guy at a party. Dark hair, dark eyes—he was a high-rise of a man, standing a good 6 inches taller than my 5-foot-10 frame. Even under a black wool sweater, he had arms that I knew could toss me into the heavens. He was incredibly handsome. I was in love. I mean lust. Whatever.

I don't remember him introducing himself. What I do remember is this: The attraction was mutual, palpable, and instantaneous. After closing down the bar, we shared a cab and exchanged numbers.

We spent the next afternoon on my sister's couch, talking backgrounds, flirting, and, eventually, talking sex. Couch time morphed into early drinks, then dinner, then more drinks at a mutual friend's apartment. A little after midnight, we broke from the group for a late-night karaoke bar, where we sat in a private room, leg over leg, on a black pleather sectional. We had no other place to go, really. He was staying with a friend. I was staying with my sister. At 3 o'clock in the morning, halfway through my painful rendition of "The Devil Went

Down to Georgia," I turned to him and said, "Let's get a hotel room."

I'd never done anything like that before. Truth is, I'd probably have thought less of any woman who had. But I'd said it, couldn't take it back, and didn't want to. He paid the tab in record speed, then pulled me off the vinyl with an audible sluuurpop! of sweaty legs. We hit the streets of Chinatown looking for the word "Vacancy."

When we finally found a room, I was the one who slid my credit card to the man behind the counter. It was my idea. There was no discussion. Boots were unzipped and shirts ripped off before the elevator reached our floor. The room was small and dirty. We were practically in the shower before the door swung closed. I'm still not sure if we were trying to wash each other of where we were or what we were about to do—or both. But as he toweled me off and swung me onto the bed, I know I had made the right decision.

He picked me up.

He didn't drop me.

Talking about sex earlier in the day, it turned out, was the best kind of foreplay. And in the hours that followed, he proved himself a great listener. I wanted to be told what to do by a partner who was physically strong enough to throw me around a little and wasn't afraid of bruises, accidental noises, rug burns, muscle aches, and sweat. Arms were held back, legs moved up, bodies flipped, turned, licked, and tucked. It was furious and unforgettable.

I'm not so naive as to think he ever wanted anything more than

Anonymous Sex "When you fantasize about a certain type of person, you lay down physical memory traces in the limbic part of your brain. When you meet that person, these pleasure centers light up. Lesson: Chemistry like this is rare. Enjoy it within boundaries that allow you to feel good about yourself in the morning." **—Daniel Amen, MD**

a one-night stand. But he skillfully played the part of my perfect lover, and in return, I played out my perfect fantasy.

Marathon Sex
The sex was endless, even if the love wasn't
By Sasha Cagen

The first time Nate and I were about to have sex, he asked me, in his goofy-cheesy way, "Do you want to make love?" If anyone else had asked me in those words, I might have burst out laughing, but Nate looked at me as if he meant it. I nodded yes, but with the familiar trepidation I feel every time a man is about to enter me the first time.

My fear is that our intercourse won't match up to what we've experienced so far; that all our fun exploration—sucking on each other's earlobes, lightly biting the small of each other's back—will fall away once we arrive at the main event. More often than not, orgasm becomes the goal. As a woman whose big O can take a while to take shape, I am often left quietly bristling with energy—while the guy beside me is spent.

With Nate, I discovered, sex would be different. Not only did it last longer, but the way he felt inside me was much more satisfying. He moved subtly, slowly, stimulating me with little circles on the left, little circles on the right, nine shallow strokes, and then a deeper thrust. There was no frantic in-out, in-out thrusting—what Carrie Bradshaw on *Sex and the City* called jackrabbit sex. He teased me with light movements. Sex was uncommonly slow, graceful, and gradual and seemed to last for hours. My mind was blown. And why did he have so much stamina?

Nate confessed: A previous girlfriend had given him a book on Taoist sexuality, an ancient Chinese school of thought that views daily lovemaking as something to cultivate not only for enjoyment but also for mental and physical health. He said *The Tao of Sexology: The Book of Infinite Wisdom* had literally changed his life.

The Taoists believe in long-lasting intercourse (as many as "one thousand loving thrusts"), that true pleasure in sex is more than a momentary sensation of release. Pleasure is defined as never being able to get enough of each other. The Chinese texts have poetic descriptions of the way Nate moved inside me: "Rise and then plunge low like a huge sailing boat braving the gale" or "Push in and out like a flock of seagulls playing on the waves."

Not only did Nate become a more considerate lover, but he also learned how to separate orgasm from ejaculation and to come more than once during sex. His orgasms were more intense, full body, and satisfying. And I was able to lose myself completely—something I had never done during sex before. My brain emptied of thoughts, my body took over—our bodies coordinated. Instead of being linear, a rote race to the finish line, undressing each other in bed was more like entering our own private world. Sex felt more creative, more open-ended, and strangely infinite. We could go as long as we wanted: 3 hours or 10 minutes. He would be inside me, then out, shimmying down my stomach, kissing me down my midriff. The man had me in a trance.

My favorite Taoist move was the simplest and least orgasm focused: the Morning Prayer. We'd assume the missionary position. Nate would use tiny movements to maintain an erection but wouldn't ejaculate. The goal was complete physical and mental connection and

Marathon Sex "From a neuroscientist's perspective, Nate was brilliant. Women want love, closeness, and someone who'll be a good father to their babies. A man who's attentive, slow, and patient, as Nate was, passes muster as both a lover and a father. Lesson: If you make her pleasure your goal, you'll enjoy yourself a lot more sexually as well." **—D.A.**

reaching a sexually meditative state. When we were together, motionless and calm, him inside me, even the smallest sensation felt very big.

Nate used to joke that any couple who practiced Morning Prayer daily would never break up. I wish it were true. If our relationship outside the bedroom had meshed half as well as the one inside, we might have been partners for life.

Breakup Sex
I hated him. I had to have him
By Tobin Levy

Jim and I had been together for 2 months when we bought our tickets to Southeast Asia. Three weeks into our 3-month adventure, it was apparent that my boyfriend hated a lot of things about me—my affinity for stray animals, my small talk, the way I looked—things that were never going to change.

The relationship ended after our sojourn through parts of Thailand, Cambodia, Vietnam, and Laos. We were in the Laos airport, heading back to Thailand, when he said the words "It's over." We parted ways, and it was Jim's imperative that we not see each other until our departure date nearly a month away.

A week later, I was in Koh Lanta, a Thai island on the Andaman Sea, when he showed up at my bungalow. "I met the laziest kitty in Koh Chang," he said, trying to make nice with an animal story.

There was a full moon that night. Thailand is known for its full-moon beach parties—with exotic music and even more exotic dancing—so we made our way down to the shore. At 4 in the morning, after deciding we'd had enough trance music for a lifetime, Jim and I started walking up the beach. When we could no long hear the umph-umph-umph reverberating from speakers, we stopped. The sea was breaking on rock formations that under the full moon's light were the most beautiful blue-black I'd ever seen. I looked at Jim with his G.I. Joe buzz cut, his pale blue eyes, and, below his left eye, the mole that I'd always loved even if I never loved him. He was standing between the water and me, his face a perfect silhouette against a starry sky.

Then the harsh realities of who he was, of who we were together, rushed in. I remembered the gastrointestinal trauma I'd experienced in Phnom Penh and how Jim had scolded me with 3 days of silence for vocalizing my pain. Then there was our impromptu expedition to Battambong, Cambodia's third-largest city and home to the one hotel touted in *Lonely Planet* for its offerings of free porn. Jim was enthusiastic, and I was determined to add spark to our rapidly dwindling sex life—but it was a bust. The hotel and the porn were both a little too seedy—too much yellow track lighting in the former and too much bondage in the latter. "Just because the porn sucks doesn't mean we can't have sex," I said. "I'm tired," he replied, then turned over and fell asleep.

There were an impossible number of recollections like these, but their severity dulled against a backdrop that included a full moon, a dramatic seascape, and a handsome, half-naked man.

Jim was soon pulling off his swim trunks and heading for the sea. I stuffed my miniskirt, tank top, and bikini under his pile of clothes and joined him in the warm water. It was so salty that floating was effortless. Jim grabbed me from behind and turned me around so I could wrap my legs around him. He was standing, holding me up. We'd made out like this on another island in a different body of water

Breakup Sex "Sex is a stew of many different feelings. This experience was about lust, loneliness, and a way to say good-bye. The writer knew there was no love when she realized she was solely concerned with her own pleasure. Lesson: Women can be as sexually selfish as men; that's okay, as long as you don't find yourself wanting more." **—D.A.**

weeks earlier, only now we weren't dating any longer. We were waiting to go back to the States so that we could become strangers. The kissing was familiar and furious, the culmination of weeks of resentment that the person with whom we'd gone on this trip wasn't whom we'd hoped for. We stayed in the water until the sun started to rise.

When we got out, the cool air was exhilarating. We laughed hysterically as we struggled into our clothes so that we could run back to my room and tear them off each other again.

The lights were dim. The pinks and oranges from the sunrise were seeping through our windows. The sex was fueled by a detached, energetic fury. It was raw sex—the kind you can have with a lover only when there is no love. We were free to be selfish, and in being selfish we were both satisfied. It was breakup, not makeup, sex. Still, I went to sleep happy.

Shameless Sex

He turned this good girl bad

By Nicole Beland

When I started hooking up as a teenager, it was with all the hell-bent fervor for which Catholic-school girls are famous. Even so, orgasm has never come easily. Perhaps that's why, as an adult, I've continued my quest for exceptional sex. I've bribed security guards so that my boyfriend and I could have a half hour of privacy on the rooftop of a Manhattan skyscraper. I've scheduled a ski vacation to coincide with the full moon so that fooling around in the Jacuzzi would be more romantic. I practice bizarre yoga positions, hoping they'll lead to bizarre sex positions.

So it's ironic that the best sex of my life took place in an ordinary bedroom on an otherwise boring Tuesday night and didn't include anything kinky. What made the encounter so memorable was simple orgasm, and then another, and then another, and then another. It was the first time a man had given me multiple orgasms. I came four times over the course of a single glorious hour.

My boyfriend, John, is a guitarist. He lives up to every woman's fantasy about musicians: He is very good with his hands. His fingers just don't quit. He's innovative, too, frequently surprising me with new moves. But what I like best is that he gives me permission to be bad. When I'm struggling to hit my peak, he whispers something dirty in my ear, forces his tongue into my mouth and pushes it around, or gives my butt a few solid slaps.

On that particular Tuesday night, we had just had sex, and I was enjoying the last waves of an orgasm. I was satisfied and assumed the fun was over. Then John flashed me a mischievous smile and slid his hand between my legs. He kissed me and gently pulled on my nipples, and soon the nerves in my lower body began to hum. Before long, I came again. After a few minutes, he rolled me on top of him and started thrusting upward, encouraging me to grind my way to number three. My clitoris felt like a fuse that had been blown. My heart was pounding, my hair was wet with sweat, and my body was tingling. Collapsing onto the bed, I was literally panting with pleasure when he kissed his way down my breasts and belly and started licking me very softly until I screamed, "Oh my God!" all the way to the end of the orgasm number four. (By the way, Sister Margaret, it was actually John I was referring to.)

Shameless Sex "Feelings of guilt—stemming from religion or memories of a bad experience—can become set in the memory centers of the brain, preventing some women from letting go. Lesson: Identify sexual roadblocks, and overwrite bad messages with more powerful memories you create by putting her pleasure first." **—D.A.**

Illicit Sex

He wasn't my husband. That was the point

By Deja Dunn

Jack and I had lusted after each other at various work functions. I was an artsy theater type; he, a natty, well-heeled philanthropist. Both of us were sexual hunters ill suited to the confines of our unhappy marriages, and we were both open to . . . something.

Jack made me feel good. While my husband constantly chided me to lose weight, Jack loved me for my voluptuous self. We flirted, gossiped, and, in truth, had already tipped into bed on various unplanned occasions. Okay, bed is a misrepresentation. We'd indulged our private passions most often in public places: abandoned nooks in hotel ballrooms, on his desk, under the stage after a performance.

One night, early in our affair, we agreed to a dinner at a friend's horse farm. In the candlelit dining room, our host regaled us with tales of horse breeding—how "teaser stallions" are deployed to arouse the mares and test their readiness for breeding, only to be substituted with fine breeding stallions at the last minute. A breeder can't risk injuring the mare during foreplay, and stallions, like most males, are always game for a little rough play with a new and willing mate.

Amid the whirl of wine and chatter, I felt my body tingling and heat rising on my cheeks. I excused myself and walked outside, feigning the effects of too much wine; within minutes, Jack stood next to me. He took my hand, and we walked toward the curving white fence that outlined the corrals. We climbed over it, dropping into the pasture. Jack immediately backed me up against the rails and kissed me feverishly.

That's when the beasts began to gallop.

Their insistent whinnying reverberated across the moist grass. As they drew closer, we felt the ground tremble. Jack pushed aside my gauzy shirt and pulled down my panties; I tugged furiously at his shirt. He slammed me against the fence. I was lost to his insistent embrace. The night had gone inky black, and I was pinioned on the fence as Jack entered me with a nearly primordial hunger. His kisses were like anesthesia; I felt numb, lost. My hair snagged on the fence, and I imagined it mingling with lost strands from the manes of fillies rubbing here and there in their own raptures. All the while, the stallions galloped around us, snorting wildly.

When we were finished, we returned to the house. They all knew. We were sweat covered and sex flushed, visibly rocked. The ruckus in the pasture was abating, and I poured myself a glass of champagne before, at last, I reclined on the couch, listening to small talk.

Illicit Sex "The biggest sex organ of all is the brain, and 30 percent of it is dedicated to vision. The encounter was set up by the visual setting of the party, the corral, and the metaphors of horse breeding. Lesson: When you talk dirty to your partner, use visual metaphors. The writer strikes me as an adrenaline junkie. Women like her are easy to find but hard to keep." **—D.A.**

QUICKIES

Translating Her Trickle, or Flood, of Tears

IDENTIFIABLE-CAUSE TEARS. I'm sad (you dumped me; my goldfish died). I'm relieved (you took me back; my goldfish pulled through). I'm experiencing vicarious emotion (Big left Carrie; my friend's goldfish died). I'm touched (that's the most beautiful thing I've ever heard!). I feel hopeless (something really big went really wrong; I have a huge zit). Say, "Why the tears? Tell me about it." Hugs help. Owen Wilson/Ben Stiller comedies help.

I-CAN'T-HANDLE-THIS TEARS. Some people deal well with conflict and arguments. I cry. Stop yelling at me, jackass.

EVERY-FOURTH-TUESDAY TEARS. My hormone-induced tears are usually totally irrational: Everything!" is wrong, yet nothing specific is wrong. Don't act as if you understand; you don't. I will, however, really try not to be quite so psycho in the future if you bring me a chocolate milk shake, then leave me alone. Note: Never be the one to suggest that a woman's tears are hormone-related. Occa-

> **INSTANT SEXPERT**
>
> **32%** of Americans say they're "very happy"; **56%**, "pretty happy."
>
> The typical American adult has sex **2 or 3** times a month.
>
> The "happiness–maximizing" number of sexual partners per year: **1**
>
> Marriage increases happiness twice as much as having sex **4** times a week does.
>
> In the entire US population, **6%** of adults say they have sex **4 or more** times a week.
>
> **22%** of American adults report having no sex.
>
> Of people who had no sex last year, only **23%** reported being "very happy," compared with **32%** of the whole sample.
>
> Greater income causes a **0%** increase in number of sexual partners and frequency of sex.

sionally, women are upset for legitimate reasons, and we hate it when men assume it's just because we're PMS-ing.

OFFICE TEARS. Crying in the office, in front of my boss, is the worst workplace disaster I can imagine—worse than puking in front of coworkers. Not that I've done that (twice). But I have cried. I screwed up big-time on a project, and I felt like a failure professionally—and, worse, personally. That's when I cry. Then I'll immediately feel stupid, weak, "like a girl." If you're my boss, show you understand. Wait a few hours—days, if possible—to discuss "how we could work together to fix it." (FYI: If the deluge returns three or more times, you might want to reconsider the employee's job tasks—or the employee.)

SEX TEARS. Crying is a mysterious release, sort of like an orgasm, which may explain why the two activities sometimes occur in near succession. Crying during sex is usually about intimacy—as in, I'm feeling so very close to you that I'm able to completely let go and express this burst of pure joy. But, in rare instances, it could be about lack of intimacy, too. Either way, I don't want to talk about it. Hold me.

MANIPULATIVE TEARS. Who, me? Okay, there may have been at least one time when I happened to cry. And that one time may or may not have been the same one time I happened to slip out of a traffic ticket and points on my license while also getting the cop's phone number. I may or may not feel guilty about this. Sometimes a girl just needs to work it. —Lisa Jones

PICK-UP TRICKS

Forget a puppy, baby, or guitar—use girl power. A woman is the best date magnet. A "wingwoman" offers something that a wingman can't—credibility. "Women are more likely to trust other women," says anthropologist Helen Fisher, PhD. Bring along an outgoing female friend who can tell the woman who's caught your eye, "He'd kill me for doing this, but my friend thinks you're beautiful. Any chance you'd join us for a drink?" Or, you can hire one for $50 an hour at wingwomen.com. Entrepreneur Shane Forbes says he started the site after noticing that "I met more attractive, available women with my female friends by my side."

THE WORLD'S BEST AND WORST LOVERS

Nearly 40 percent of women worldwide say they have faked an orgasm in the past year, according to research from the 2004 Durex Global Sex Survey. Check out the map to see how often women are having real ones—and where men are getting the job done.

Percentage of women who report having an orgasm during sexual intercourse in:

ITALY
29%: Every time
41%: Almost every time

CHINA
11%: Every time
21%: Almost every time

BRAZIL
22%: Every time
35%: Almost every time

JAPAN
8%: Every time
25%: Almost every time

UNITED KINGDOM
16%: Every time
33%: Almost every time

CANADA
14%: Every time
37%: Almost every time

SOUTH AFRICA
19%: Every time
39%: Almost every time

UNITED STATES
17%: Every time
31%: Almost every time

ASK THE GIRL NEXT DOOR
The honest truth about women from our lovely neighbor

XXX-planation
Why do women mind if their men look at porn? —R.J., MORGANTOWN, WV

Probably because we seldom use porn ourselves. Blame it on how we were raised. A female-friendly skin mag is never slipped to girls with an approving nudge by older members of the field-hockey team or with a wink and a smile by a randy aunt. Most women I know didn't start masturbating until well into their twenties. Parents and teachers taught us that porn is dirty and shameful. So that's the way many women still look at it, instead of as what it really is—a quick release of sexual tension that doesn't require thought or emotion. Look on the bright side: If porn ever became completely socially acceptable, it wouldn't work as well.

Cheaters Never Win
Would you give a man a second chance if he cheated on you?
—MATTHEW, CHAPEL HILL, NC

Look, I'm no angel—I cheated once. I know how tempting it is to give in to a visceral urge. I also know it's possible to have a sexual encounter that involves little or no emotion. But my answer is still no. I wouldn't give a guy a second chance because, at this point in my life, I'm willing to do the hard stuff—to be honest and faithful and make sacrifices. Being with just one person is difficult, maybe even unnatural. That's why being faithful is such an incredible gift. If I'm going to all the trouble of giving that gift, I sure as hell want to get it in return.

Give Good Gift

How can I impress my wife for our next wedding anniversary?

—MARTIN, ROYAL OAK, MI

Wow her—and make every anniversary easier—with this romantic move: Suggest starting a tradition. Send your wife a card a few weeks before your anniversary, inviting her to meet you at the fanciest restaurant in town. Show up in a suit, order a bottle of champagne, and make a toast to the love of your life. Have the waiter bring out a dessert with a candle in it, then stand up, walk over, and kiss her before she blows it out. If you're an understated, practical guy, that's impressive enough.

If she's used to more creativity, hand her a leather-bound photo album filled with pictures of the two of you from the past year. If you can afford it, upgrade to a weekend at a gorgeous hotel in one of her favorite cities. Tell her you'd like to celebrate your anniversary this way every year. If she agrees, you never have to wonder what to do again.

Bedroom Critique

Is there any right way to tell a woman that the sex wasn't good for me?   —MIKE, VIA E-MAIL

No. Most women are so self-conscious in bed that they can't even have an orgasm in the first place. Tell your partner that sex with her is only so-so, and she may never recover. Since women become better in bed the more confident they feel, criticism is counterproductive to creating a sex kitten. Instead, passionately praise the one or two things she happens to do well, then offer soft-spoken, playful suggestions about the moves you'd like her to try. Take turns performing the same sexual favor on each other. Go first and show her what you like by example (or at least by approximate example). During sex, say things like, "Wow, that feels amazing. I bet it would feel crazy good if you did it a little softer/harder/faster/slower." But whatever you do, don't be negative—unless you want to see a naked woman cry.

The Executive Love Letter

I'm in love with our senior vice president of finance. I know it's ridiculous, but I can't stop thinking about her. She seems to like me too. Do these things ever work out? —ANONYMOUS, PLANO, TX

No. Except when they do. Try having sex in the office at night, when everybody else is gone. It's terrific.

I'm assuming several things, by the way: 1. You're correct in your feeling that she likes you too. 2. You're neither junior nor senior to this lovely colleague. These romances only make sense when they involve peers. Anything else is an engraved invitation to the slammer, chum. 3. She's not married and you aren't either, although to tell you the truth, that's less important from a professional point of view. It's just good advice. Unless you're a thrill junkie.

In that regard, try going on the road together now and then. A snowy night in Dubuque can feel like Paris in February if you're with the right corporate officer.

Sexual Wheeling

My wife uses sex as a bargaining tool, which doesn't seem fair. How do I get her to stop? —NAME WITHHELD

How are your thespian skills? Pretend you're some B actor in a sappy Lifetime movie and say this like you mean it: "The way you hold sex over my head is damaging the intimacy of our relationship." Explain that when she treats "making love" like anything other than something "fun and exciting and romantic," it becomes "emotionally empty"—which bothers you because you want making love with her to be "positive and meaningful." Don't worry—she'll understand what you're talking about even if you don't. And you'll also be speaking the truth.

TWO WORLDS COLLIDE

Boy meets girl. Boy kisses girl. Girl dumps boy with no real explanation. If this sounds familiar to you, you could be missing some key moves that could help you change the last sentence of that story to something like " . . . and they lived happily ever after."

In the first two parts of this book, you learned some things about yourself and about women. Now it's time to learn how to play the game—and play it with skill. In the pages to follow, you'll learn what to wear, what to say, where to take her (hint: not a strip club!), and how to keep her. Find out what charms her and what makes her head straight for the door. You've got the skills—here's the game plan!

The 10 Best Things Ever Said about Hooking Up

1. Nobody will ever win the battle of the sexes. There's too much fraternizing with the enemy. —HENRY KISSINGER

2. Our courtship was fast and furious—I was fast and she was furious. —MAX KAUFMANN

3. I wanna die with you Wendy on the streets tonight/In an everlasting kiss. —BRUCE SPRINGSTEEN

4. Love is the delusion that one woman is different from another. —HL MENCKEN

5. The best love affairs are those we never had.
—NORMAN LINDSAY

6. A man falls in love through his eyes, a woman through her ears. —WOODROW WYATT

7. Lots of women go out with me just to further their careers—damn anthropologists! —EMO PHILIPS

8. It is strange, the stages by which you realize you are too late—you have swallowed the hook. —JOHN HERMAN

9. Love is a rose but you better not pick it/ It only grows when it's on the vine. —NEIL YOUNG

10. Men play the game; women know the score.
—ROGER WODDIS

How to Dress for a Date

We polled the pros, combed the journals, and checked out the stats. The results: Eight scientific principles of dressing that leave nothing to chance

BY LISA JONES

WOO HER WITH FRAGRANCE

"Women have a better sense of smell than men do, and it's even sharper in the middle of their menstrual cycle, when estrogen levels peak and women are more likely to be deciding whether a man's attractive," says Helen Fisher, PhD, a professor of anthropology at Rutgers University and the author, most recently, of *Why We Love*. Wearing fragrant leather is one great way to get inside her head.

- To encourage her animal instincts, wear the hide of a beast, and maintain it well. Preserving its oils releases natural fragrance.

EXPLORE THE VERTICAL

Women rate tall men as more sexually attractive than shorter guys, and tall men are more likely to find a mate. Proof: A British study of more than 10,000 people found that men 6 feet tall were more likely than average-height men (5'10") to be married and have children.

- Wear pinstripes. Vertical lines enhance your height, and it's easier than standing on your toes.

CONVEY STATUS

We all know what you're looking for when you check out a woman. You dog. But that doesn't mean she's looking for sex signifiers when

Clear Signals

It turns out you can just sit there on a bar stool and attract women—but it depends on how you sit. A recent study in the journal *Evolution and Human Behavior* found that the men who are the most successful with women exhibit a certain body language before they make their approach. Check out the most effective nonverbal pickup language.

Open Body Positioning

Men who have open body language—who don't close off their torsos with crossed arms—are seen as more attractive, potent, active, and persuasive.

Space-Maximization Movement

The most dominant man in a group commands the most space. Men who stretch or extend their arms and legs across chairs convey control of personal and physical space.

Intrasexual Touching

Touching your guy friends (within limits, of course) shows affection. Touchers are perceived as having more status and more social power than those being touched—or those who don't touch at all.

Glancing Behavior

Men who frequently glance around are more likely to make eye contact with women—and women respond better to men with whom they've already exchanged glances.

she scopes you out. A study of mate selection in 37 cultures found that women seek partners with status, class, and success. So she's looking for a bulge in your pants, all right—the one made by your wallet. "Now, this doesn't mean that every woman wants a businessman from New York City," says Fisher. "But if she walks into a bar and there are three accountants and one is wearing a nicer suit, she might notice it and be attracted to that man. Women like signs of money and education—things that indicate that not only is this guy going to have some resources but he's also willing to share them."

- Spend, and spend some more, on watches and cool shoes. They're the first two stops on her itinerary.

SHOW OFF YOUR TESTOSTERONE

"Women are looking for men with good genes so their children can have good genes," says Devendra Singh, PhD, a professor of psychology at the University of Texas. One thing they're noticing, probably without realizing it, is a man's waist-to-hip ratio. In cross-cultural studies, women rate men with 0.8 to 0.95 ratios (almost a straight line) as most appealing. "Women are unconsciously performing these calculations—judging men on the basis of how body fat is distributed," she says. The ratio is an indicator of testosterone. Testosterone inhibits fat in the buttocks and waist but allows it in the upper body, explains Singh. So when a man has a large waist or butt, it indicates low testosterone, and a woman will consider him less attractive.

- Don't leave home without a sport coat. It creates a visual line from your neck to your thighs, which conveys an appealing waist-to-hip ratio, according to Michael Cunningham, PhD, who studies attraction at the University of Louisville.
- Unless you regularly appear on the cover of this magazine, avoid anything cinched or tightly belted at the waist.

GIVE GOOD FACE

Pure animal attraction is linked to your face and its symmetry. Sixty-five studies of 42 species have connected symmetry and sex appeal, according to the *Penguin Atlas of Human Sexual Behavior*. In addition, the better a man's symmetry, the more quickly he gets women into bed, the more sexual partners he has, and the more orgasms he causes in women partners, according to the atlas. You can't change your face (at least not without a scalpel), but you can frame it properly.

- Wear a straight-point-collar dress shirt, with collar points $2^3/_4$ to 3 inches in length. This collar frames the face best and with the least margin of error for most men, regardless of face shape, says Alan Flusser, men's-fashion expert and author of *Dressing the Man*. When you're not wearing a tie, unbutton the top one or two buttons.

PROJECT STRENGTH

Broad shoulders connote strength and confidence—and 22 percent of women in a British study rated them as men's sexiest body part.

- Wear a shirt with raglan sleeves (diagonal seams from the armpit to the neck). Ballplayers wear 'em, and they routinely reach third base.

DISPLAY YOUR TRUE COLORS

"Women have a better sense of color and a better color memory," says Fisher. "They're more likely to notice when something doesn't match and more likely to notice what you're wearing." Use different colors to convey different desirable personality traits and to evoke different feelings in your date.

- Surrender to pink. "It's a color women gravitate toward," says Lisa Herbert, an executive vice president at Pantone, a leading color-research firm. "It indicates intimacy and sensitivity."
- Not ready for pink? Meet her halfway with purple, which combines the masculinity and stability of blue with the softness of pink, says Herbert.
- Encourage a crush: Wear orange. "It's very outgoing and high energy," says Herbert. "For an active date, we would recommend wearing a really bright orange."

GO SKIN TO SKIN

Your first mission on a date (indeed, the key to all subsequent missions) is contact: Get her to touch you. "Touch is the mother of the senses," says Fisher. "Not only are women more sensitive when they touch, but they're also more sensitive to being touched." It has to do with millions of years of nurturing behavior, explains Fisher. Women, as mothers and caretakers, use touch to identify health threats such as fever and swollen glands. Show a woman your soft side—she'll expose hers in return.

- Apply moisturizer at least twice a day, and if you must cover skin, do it with touchable all-stars like cashmere, pima cotton, brushed corduroy, merino wool, and suede. When sex is on the line, definitely wear velvet.

Are You Trying Too Hard?

Or not hard enough? Strike the right balance and she won't be able
to keep her mind, or her hands, off you

BY SARAH MILLER

WOMEN LOVE MEN. We want your attention and love
more than we want anything else on this planet. That's the good
news. The not-so-good news is that the amount of attention and love
we want is very specific. If you don't give us enough, we will get mad
and seek it elsewhere. Shower us with too much and we lose interest,
right after we get grossed out. Striking the perfect balance makes us
feel taken care of and independent all at once, and that makes you irresistible. These 10 simple lessons will help you find the right pro-
portions.

**1. YOU'RE TRYING TOO HARD IF YOU USE ANY LINE OTHER THAN "HI, MY
NAME IS JIMMY." YOU'RE NOT TRYING HARD ENOUGH IF YOU JUST STAND
THERE AND DRINK BEER.** The first step, as always, is getting a woman to
go out with you. Whether you're talking to a friend of a friend, a
woman you met at a bar, or a photogenic stranger online, you want to
come across as interested and friendly but not desperate. You will not
lose points for approaching with confidence. Remember, women
want you to hit on them; it's why we wear tank tops and lipstick. Once
you have engaged her attention, the really hard part is over. The best
thing you can do at this point is just let her talk. She should be good
at that.

When it's your turn, try to give answers that are not mumbled
and are more detailed than a Magic 8-Ball response. Say something

about why you got into your line of work or, if you hate your job, something about your pet. If you hate your job and you don't have a pet, you must be very unhappy, so then, of course, you could start talking about therapy. The point is, you can talk about anything, and if you're funny and relatively sure of yourself, she'll appreciate your input. When in doubt, turn the focus back on her.

Also, during initial encounters, it's common for guys to start ticking off their accomplishments, such as, "It's funny you should mention your plans for the Fourth of July, because I happened to go to Harvard—near Boston, where the American Revolution began." Keep in mind that talking to a woman for the first time is not a job interview, however similar the two might seem. Excerpt your résumé sparingly.

2. YOU'RE TRYING TOO HARD IF THE EVENING YOU'VE ARRANGED RE-QUIRED MORE THAN TWO RESERVATIONS. YOU'RE NOT TRYING HARD ENOUGH IF YOU SHOW UP EXPECTING HER TO IMPROVISE A GAME PLAN. Some men make the mistake of going all out on the first date—the limo, the four-star restaurant, the front-row seats. That worked for Frank Sinatra, but unless you once sold out the Copa Room at the Sands, it will not work for you.

Lust in Translation

A recent survey shows that speaking a foreign language makes you more attractive. Now consider this: A Japanese panel of experts in psychology and sociology developed the ultimate romantic line: *Rainen no kono hi mo issho ni waratteiyoh.* Translation: "This time next year, let's be laughing together." John Nathan, PhD, a professor of Japanese cultural studies at the University of California, Santa Barbara, says the line could work in Japan but warns, "American women might be a little less gullible."

If such luxury is not your standard, you're going to be out of your element at a time when you should be smack in its middle. Stick with what you know. Take her to a place you like, where the owner and host and waitstaff know you. Familiarity and friendliness impress us, unless it's a topless bar.

And don't forget: Clean your car. If you invite her back to your place at the end of the evening and your home is a little messy, that's not such a big deal. (You might even get bonus points because it will appear that your proposition wasn't premeditated.) A messy car, however, is a different story. Something about it just says, "I want to be alone. Forever."

3. SMITTEN CAN EASILY TURN INTO PATHETIC. It's natural, in the heat of a new relationship, to go wild. You want to whisk her away for a romantic weekend; you want to create brilliant mix CDs for her; you want to pull her into every available photo booth for cute snapshots of the two of you nuzzling. And if you're pretty sure she's 100 percent into you, go for it. (Just don't make us watch.) If, however, you sense that she's interested, yet not quite as over the moon as you are, try doing one of those things, but not all of them.

See, you shouldn't be afraid to try to win over a woman who's undecided about you; if it didn't occasionally work, the word "woo" wouldn't exist. But if you must pursue, do so without getting all neurotic about it and simply because you enjoy the pleasure of her company. Most women find such pure dedication difficult to ignore.

Tip: Don't ever ask a woman you're dating, "Where is this going?" If you have to ask, the answer is not likely to be one you'll want to hear. And anyway, women have exclusive rights to that query, don't ya know?

4. WHEN IT COMES TO SEX, HER SAYING "WOW" IS GOOD. "WOW, ARE YOU AUDITIONING FOR THE CIRCUS?" MEANS YOU PROBABLY NEED TO EASE IT DOWN A NOTCH. Women do like to have orgasms. We don't need to have 10 in one night. Secret, exciting techniques are great; if they're effective, it will be evident and there will be no need for a recap, complete with anatomy lesson, of what just transpired. The good thing about sex is that it's intimate. The scary thing is that intimacy brings out everyone's insecurities. Avoid the impulse to ask if it was good, and how good, and was it the best? As for trying to find out what she likes, you should be able to tell by her responses.

If you're not sure, say something like, "Just FYI, I take requests." Add a wink, and an icky conversation is successfully avoided.

Don't ask, "Did you enjoy that?" You'll sound like a waiter—a particularly annoying waiter, at that.

5. COMMUNICATION: GOOD. POETRY: BAD. My friend received an e-mail from her new boyfriend the other day that said, "I'm watching the skies of Seattle grayen and begin to weep, and taking some time to reflect on the day." This is a classic example of a guy trying way, way too hard. I don't know if she's broken up with him yet, but she's probably thinking about it. What's sad is that some ex-girlfriend probably told him he should share his feelings more, but then neglected to add that those feelings should be expressed in plain English and not dressed up in a stupid little outfit. Women really want to hear absolutely everything, so talk, fax, e-mail, call us all you want. But when you do, make sure you sound genuine.

Rule of thumb: You know you're in trouble when you start making up words.

6. THINK BOYFRIEND, NOT BUTLER. Men with good manners are cute and can even be sexy. Men with excessively good manners are obsequious and often repulsive. It's a question of degree: If it's raining or she's wearing a formal gown, go ahead and open her car door first; otherwise, it's fine, after the first few dates, to just unlock it from inside. Getting her a drink from the bar is great, but don't order dinner for her. Opening doors is nice, but not if you have to sprint ahead of her to do so. Leaving her at the coffee shop while you run to the deli for the soy milk she likes or mailing a shower puff to her at the office

Charm a Cat Woman

Be her pet. Dogs are easy to like—they look cool catching a Frisbee. But if the girl who's got you panting has a cat (75 percent of cat owners are women), try to make nice with these feline-taming tips.

Don't chase tail. "It's a mistake to pursue a cat too aggressively," says veterinarian Lore Haug, of Texas A&M University. "Let the cat decide when it wants to be petted. It will let you know."

Skip the scent. Lay off the cologne and cigarettes. Strong odors can freak out a feline.

Bring treats. If the cat can smell the goodies on you, it will want to be near you. Oh, and bring flowers for the owner. Cats are very sensitive to their owners' emotions. If Mama's happy, Kitty's happy.

Invade her territory. Find the sofa pillow or chair covered with fur—that's the cat's spot. Eventually, it'll crawl up next to you. Scratch it gently on the neck and behind the ears, and wait for its mistress to join you.

because she mentioned in passing that she needs a new one (true stories) is way too attentive.

Relax. We're not expecting too much. Show us just a degree more courtesy than you'd show the next guy, and you'll impress.

7. GO THE FUN—NOT ROMANTIC WITH A CAPITAL R—ROUTE FOR A FIRST-TIME GETAWAY. Flying to Paris with a man sounds romantic to a woman. Your mentioning it on date three sounds moderately psycho—and a lot like a false promise. When you first knock suitcases with a new lover, make sure they're weekender bags—and drive to a nearby casual destination. Heading to Texas for your cousin's wedding: not so casual.

Side note: If you're both outdoorsy and athletic, an adventurous weekend spent rafting or rock climbing will show off your muscles and be sure to impress. However, if you lack athletic grace, it's a bad idea to ask a woman you've just started seeing to go on, say, a ski weekend. Your sitzmark won't be sexy. Her fake fall to ease your embarrassment won't be subtle. Everyone will end up bruised and turned off.

8. YOU'RE TRYING TOO HARD IF YOU TAKE HER HOME TO MAMA TOO SOON. YOU'RE NOT TRYING HARD ENOUGH IF SHE SUSPECTS YOU'RE AN OR-PHAN. It's okay—good, even—to talk about your family on early dates. It helps us create the emotional profile of you that we're building in our minds. But it's scary to a woman if you let slip too early that you told your mom about her, or if you ask her to meet your parents before it's clear you're an exclusive couple.

Tip: Family photos on your fridge can launch intimate conversations. However, nonstop chatter about your nieces and nephews says you're trying too hard to appear being really into kids. This tends to be a common tip-off of commitment phobia. Consider yourself suspect.

9. RANDOM ACTS OF KINDNESS IMPRESS. DOING EVERYTHING FOR HER IS PATRONIZING. Changing the lightbulb in her high-ceilinged kitchen because you've noticed it's been out for a while and, well, you know she can't reach it and has a fear of ladders is the kind of stealth thoughtful move that makes a girl want to keep you around forever. Changing all the bulbs in her apartment to energy-saving fluorescent: trying too hard. Yes, women love men who volunteer their strength and guy knowledge when needed and, sometimes, without asking. The fact that you want to take care of her is sexy.

But bear in mind: She managed her life before you came along.

10. REMEMBER: YOUR COUSIN VICTOR, WHO ACTS LIKE A JERK BUT HAS NINE GIRLFRIENDS, IS NOT A ROLE MODEL. HE'S A FORCE OF NATURE. Yes, there are guys out there who treat women poorly and still get laid all the time. You wonder, *Would I have better luck if I behaved the way* *they do?* You wouldn't. And here's why: Those guys are either really gorgeous or otherwise oozing some mysterious sex appeal that can be neither identified nor emulated. Sorry. Someday those men will be old and will not, like you, have cultivated all these amazing woman-pleasing skills. Their beautiful young wives will cheat on them with the next generation of sex-seeping slimeballs. Take comfort in this.

In the meantime: You're sentenced to a romantic life demanding a healthy modicum of effort, many acts of kindness, and occasional restraint. Start now!

What I Learned at the Strip Club

There just may be more to it than beers, leers, and lap dances

BY THOMAS BELLER

I **TOLD MY GIRLFRIEND** I was going to write about strip clubs.

"When did you last go to one?" she asked.

"A few years ago."

She gave me one of those long, baleful stares whose meaning I can never be sure about, but which seemed to suggest that she had suspected something really unpleasant about me—had glimpsed it or maybe its shadow—and now, like the Loch Ness Monster rising in all its hideous glory from the deep, it stood before her in plain sight.

"Come on," I said. "What's the big deal? It's practically wholesome!"

"It is not wholesome," she said rather forcefully, and there the conversation ended, to my relief.

In the big picture, of course, I was right. In the grand scheme of grisly war footage, sex exploitation, and violence voyeurism—in which hockey fights are edited together to form one continuous face bash—a strip club is a harmless excursion, a night out with the boys.

But life is not lived in the big picture. It is lived moment to moment, and that first moment when one walks into a nudie bar is not wholesome at all. You feel lust, relief, excitement, and revulsion. The revulsion, curiously, somehow enhances the intensity of the other emotions. It's a shock in the same way jumping into the cold ocean is a shock—no matter how many times you've done it, you're never really quite prepared.

All day long—at work, around town, at the supermarket—you're surrounded by unknown breasts. They're hidden behind bras and shirts, camouflaged by hunched shoulders, protected by crossed arms. You see legs and skirts and marvel at how such thin layers of fabric separate you from the goods. Then you walk into a strip club and suddenly the curtain is lifted, the mystery revealed. Is this body exciting on its own merits or just because it can be seen? Or is it exciting because it doesn't belong to your girlfriend or wife?

It takes a few minutes to adjust, but then—as with cold water or, more apropos, a porn flick—the shock wears off, and the naked woman onstage becomes simply a woman who happens to be naked. The testosterone-soaked carnality that brought you here evaporates, and it becomes just a place, a bar. That's the odd thing about strip clubs: The reason you go is not the reason you stay because, really, strip clubs aren't about women at all.

A few years ago, two friends and I sauntered into a place called Billy's Topless in New York City. The atmosphere was no more illicit than if we had decided to go get hamburgers. My friends were regulars. One was my age, and the other, Nick, was an older man who reminded me of Dean Martin in his Rat Pack days—thin, stylish, and self-possessed.

My friend and I, the junior members of the trio, looked up to Nick in a way, because he seemed to offer a solution to the conundrum of how to acknowledge one's more perverted, voracious, and generally seedy side, yet still seem like a gentleman. He could walk to the stage and slip a dollar bill into the hand of a dancer and smile at her with such debonair ease that when, several drinks into the evening, he professed that one dancer or another was in love with him, it was possible to believe him. Of course, since he was a regular, it was an ongoing relationship he was referring to. We admired the guy, without necessarily wanting to be him. And so our evening had as much to do with Nick the diabetic drinker—he was now on club soda—as it did with the women onstage.

Strip clubs are bastions of a kind of twisted chivalry. Undoubtedly, some men will use the transaction as a thin pretext for copping a feel or a glancing touch, but it's more common to see guys giving out dollar bills with a look of noblesse oblige. Sometimes they act as though they're presenting the stripper with a bouquet, a sign of their affection. More often they hand it over in a gesture of camaraderie: "Yeah, thanks for the fun, baby. We all have jobs."

But this gesture is just an awkward attempt to hold on to the self most people see out in the world. The moment you enter, you're awakened from your civilized slumber and reminded of the style in which you want to f————and what a gross pig you can be. All the dormant, free-floating sexual aggression that's been hovering in the back of your mind all day, making little cameo appearances in your imagination at staggeringly inappropriate moments, now springs into action and takes over your brain. It's a release—and a relief.

Most men manage to be gentlemen in a strip club, at least for a while; it's really a question of pride. You're in a strip club, but you don't want to seem desperate, even to yourself. But once in a while, your other incarnation comes out—the lust-struck inebriate, who is the embodiment of a pathetic weakness to which everyone present can, on at least a tiny level, relate.

For every nine guys who seem under control, there is invariably one man with a craven expression of desire on his face, who wants dearly to engage this writhing creature onstage in the carnal scenarios he's been concocting at the bar. This man is not just having a good time, drinking and collecting mental souvenirs to be used during some future sex fantasy—he wants to make it happen now. Really. You can see it in his eyes. This guy is not necessarily bad-looking, though there are always some amazingly pathetic-looking men in strip clubs: worshipful, bitter, ugly, and bent by the effects of going too long without human contact. The impossibility of this contact makes the spectacle better and worse at once, by which I mean more interesting and more painful to watch.

The idea that the stripper actually likes you is a delusion I've veered precariously near on a few occasions. Alcohol abets it a great deal. Most men become sentimental and romantic when they get drunk. They want their lives to look pretty, to have architecture. With just a little wishful thinking, you grow convinced that the naked woman onstage thinks you are attractive and wants to talk to you. The problem is that it can be hard to finesse these emotions. When drunk, you're like a recreational sailor who pilots his little Sunfish into the deep water for fun but is buffeted by severe winds. The waves are higher than you thought. You lose control.

One minute you're engaging in some harmless fantasy, and the next you're staggering to the pulpit and handing over a dollar, your expression that of a deer blinded by headlights. You try to act composed: Strippers are women, after all, and if you want to get to know them as women, as opposed to anatomically correct, moving mannequins, you need to somehow get past this awkward situation in which you are sliding a dollar into a girl's G-string. So you make a joke or say something sincere, something honest and flattering, and indulge in the high-school fantasy that the class beauty will suddenly awaken one morning and realize that you, among all your varsity-football-playing classmates, are in fact the most desirable boy.

The stripper's response to this is to smile in a kind of sisterly, amused way or to just playact at whatever role she wants. Or, quite often, to retreat into a tiny, self-enclosed space of self-regard. Strip clubs' stages are always backed with mirrors—more for the strippers than for the patrons, who must avoid them lest they catch a glimpse of that extremely unerotic sight: themselves. The mirror is the stripper's friend, and often she will spend a lot of time staring into it, examining herself in a matter-of-fact, slightly curious way, watching herself dance.

This gaze is her statement of intent, as if to make it clear that the only person she truly cares about pleasing is the one she sees in the mirror, so you might as well get lost. This is what snaps you back to reality.

There used to be a seedy little topless bar near my apartment in Manhattan, across the street from a nursery (for plants, not kids). I'd drop by now and then after a long night out, sometimes with friends, sometimes without. Once, I was walking down the street with a friend and his girlfriend, and when we passed the place, she said she wanted to go in.

We were caught off guard. We made her promise that if she felt the slightest bit uncomfortable, she'd say so and we'd leave. When we walked in, I immediately started playing a video game, my back to the stage, as if I couldn't bear to see what was there to be seen. My friend hung nearby, as his girlfriend went deeper into the room to find a table. A minute into the game, my friend grabbed my arm, panicked.

"We have to leave right now," he said.

I turned, expecting to see his girlfriend in tow. But she wasn't there. He pointed down the length of the bar, where she sat beneath a gyrating stripper, her face as pale as the stripper's ass and fixed in horror. She was having a bad trip, and we had to grab her and evacuate. For the rest of the night, she acted as if she'd endured a brief bout of food poisoning.

I know there are some girls—strippers, for example—who don't find such environments a big deal, for whom a strip club has a certain noir charm. But even if my friend's girlfriend had been one of them— even if she'd been sliding dollars into some girl's G-string—we would have had to leave. The dynamic was all wrong. It was uncomfortable. This was not a place for girlfriends.

That's the contrarian reality of strip clubs: The most fun to be had is with other guys. It's the last men's club. This place, where guys go for the explicit purpose of staring at long legs and naked breasts, is one of the few remaining places men can go to not think about women.

Do You Dare?

The typical American male thinks about kinky sex but rarely does anything about it. That may change—tonight. Our exclusive poll of 2,131 women reveals some surprising desires

BY GRANT STODDARD

T HE WORD CAN CONJURE UP unsavory images: leather-clad ne'er-do-wells brandishing whips, emotionally crippled Dungeons and Dragons aficionados prancing in military regalia. The Gimp in *Pulp Fiction*.

It makes you stop and wonder, who needs to go to all that trouble? And why?

Most of us men are simple creatures. We know what we like, and we like what we know. So we're reluctant to to replace a good old-fashioned horizontal bop with a session that requires a trunkful of apparatus, significant prep time, and possibly a run to the drugstore.

On the other hand, can't there be wholesome kink? Somthing cleaner, less coercive and more collaborative, more fun and less frightening? Like, say, your woman, dressed as a cheerleader, behind the stadium with you. That's role playing and mild exhibitionism. Work for you? Thought so.

I was a man of simple pleasures until, through a twisted twist of fate, I found myself a reluctant (really!) participant in an orgy. Within a week, I became the world's unlikeliest sex columnist, for Nerve.com. After more than 30 truly kinky adventures—some of which I liked, many that still give me night terrors—I can report that I'm no Caligula. But the experiences taught me that an occasional adventure in the bedroom (or outside of it) is a great way to avoid a rut in your rutting.

Now comes the liberating news that we men are not alone in our desires. When *Men's Health* polled more than 2,000 *Cosmopolitan* readers, we learned that women are waiting for us to suggest a few deviations from the norm. Our favorite stat: More than 90 percent of women sound eager—they're "game to try" something kinky (70 percent) or downright "excited" at the prospect (21.5 percent), if only we'd ask!

If it helps, don't call it kink. "Think of it as fun—a romp, really—more than kinky," says Sue Johanson, a sex educator and the host of *Talk Sex* with Sue Johanson, on the Oxygen Network.

Consider this a fun starter guide to kink's simpler pleasures—and leave the truly freaky stuff to the Germans.

BDSM

Don't let the unsexy acronym put you off. BDSM stands for bondage, domination, submission, and masochism. For now let's address the B and a little D, which are more popular than you might think. I have yet to meet a woman who has not enjoyed being tied to a headboard now and then. Amanda, a 27-year-old advertising sales woman, is typical: "I'm a pretty confident, successful career woman. The feeling of being helpless and dominated was really novel and a massive turn-on." Doesn't sound like your girl? You'd be surprised. The women in our poll rate bondage as the form of nontraditional sex that most excites them.

"There is a sense of being erotically overwhelmed that comes along with being restrained, and many women find it quite passionate," says Carol Queen, PhD, staff sexologist at Good Vibrations, a woman-owned and operated sex-toy empire. "Women are encouraged to understand themselves as objects of desire, and through bondage and restraint, there's an acting out of that."

AT FIRST: During one of your typical romps, use your hands to restrain hers above her head. If she seems to like that (go ahead, ask) consider taking it further the next time around. Grab neckties, silk scarves, or a pair of stockings. Use gentle knots and give yourself access to all areas. Then resume what you were doing. Only slower.

Spanking can liven things up. "How hard one should spank depends on the person," says Emma Taylor, one-half of the sex-writing duo Em and Lo and coauthor of *Nerve's Guide to Sex Etiquette for Ladies and Gentlemen*. "Always err on the side of reserve, and gradually build up to rudeness." Start with a light tap. If she laughs, laugh along with her. Consider a moan permission to continue.

LATER: Laidie Magenta is a dominatrix in the big leagues of New York City. Heed Laidie Magenta's instructions; do not displease her: "BDSM can be dangerous if embarked upon by someone inexperienced and too eager. It's best to be prepared with some knowledge so no one gets hurt." Before you start, agree on a "safe word" to let each other know when you've had enough. "Saying no might be an integral part of the fantasy, so make sure your safe word is totally out of context," says sex educator Jamye Waxman. Like "peanut butter," "Seattle," or "toy boat." (Unless your fantasy involves all three, in which case you are no newcomer to kink.)

HER STORY: "It happened really naturally—my husband and I aren't about going out and purchasing a set of handcuffs. But one time during sex he said, 'Okay, you don't get to use your hands,' and that really added a whole new level. We would take turns: He would hold on to the headboard and I'd do my thing, then we'd switch. I like feeling that he could just have his way with me and I'd be powerless to stop him. It's total trust, and that's sexy."

—CARLEY, 26, SOCIAL WORKER

CAMERAS & ACTION

So want her to be a Hilton? Don't get your hopes up. Only 15 percent of the women in our survey had videotaped their bedroom antics, presumably because of what happened to Paris and other Web victims. That said, "to see what we look like in the heat of passion fulfills our deepest curiosity about something primal in our lives," says Candida

Royalle, author of *How to Tell a Naked Man What to Do.* You can try her line. No guarantee it'll work.

If she's skittish but cooperative, hand her the tape as soon as you're finished, or destroy it once you've had your fun with it. If it's a keeper, lock it in a seperate location, far from the VHS tapes of *Everybody Loves Raymond.*

AT FIRST: "Try forgoing the tape," says Royalle. She and her boyfriend did that after she retired from from making porn. "We would hook the camera up directly to the TV," she says, "bypassing any videotape or evidence, and be able to look over at ourselves in the heat of passion." Consider a safer still camera (digital or Polaroid), which is less intimidating to beginners.

LATER: Sex is a beautiful thing to watch. "Never use overhead lighting," says Royalle. "It creates shadows, and besides, overhead lights are just plain ugly." Robert Birch, PhD, a clinical sexologist, reminds us that while men are visually stimulated, "women are more aural. As long as there are lots of sounds, a woman can find the enjoyment."

HER STORY: "My husband and I bought a digital camera for our trip to South America. He was playing around with it in the hotel one night, and I did a silly, sexy dance with my towel as I was getting out of the shower. When we watched it, I was pleasantly surprised: It was so beautiful and, frankly, kind of hot. That inspired us to set up the camera on the nightstand while we had sex. It looked great—the camera was far enough away to avoid any gross porno shots—and it was incredibly sexy to watch. I was bummed when we had to erase it for more space to record the Incan temples."

—SUSAN, 27, ENGINEER

ROLE PLAYING

I'm not going to pretend that a self-respecting man could make it through this experiment without feeling like a complete fool. It requires a herculean suspension of disbelief—but so does watching *Weird Science,* and that doesn't make the experience any less enjoyable.

Many popular roles (boss/secretary, teacher/student, stripper/customer) play on the theme of "someone is in control, and the other is at his or her mercy." "These strong dynamics, even in healthy and fun sexual relationships," says Jean Mone, a New York City sex therapist. "They allow the woman and the man to enact their fantasies in a way that won't leave them feeling vulnerable."

AT FIRST: This doesn't have to extend outside the bedroom. "My boyfriend bought me lacy lingerie that's unlike anything I've ever worn," says Brittany, 27, a teacher. "It's not my style at all, but when I wear it, I feel like a different person in bed—sexy, crazy, empowered."

For a public thrill, go to a bar where neither of you will be recognized. Arrive 20 minutes apart and try to pick her up, pretending you've never laid eyes on each other. Have a name, occupation, and background in mind—and make it fun. Always wanted to blatantly hit on a hot stranger? Now you can. "There's something exciting about going public with our sexuality," Birch says.

LATER: Tweak the bar trick. Wear clothes she hasn't seen before and a different cologne because the sense of smell is tied closely to memory. You want her to forget who you are. And if you're used to the Four Seasons, try the Red Roof Inn.

Aim for euphoria, not hysteria. "It's okay to laugh, but it's also a good idea to feel like you're in a sexy mode," says Queen. "If the idea of putting on the pirate hat makes you giggle, bring the role play a little closer to home." You're not going for an Emmy here—just great sex.

HER STORY: "We did it as a goof, giggling when we first met at the bar. But after we realized how much the scenario was making the dynamic between us different, we quickly set the scene for some of the most memorable sex either of us has ever had. I always wanted to be a wanton slut but met my soul mate when I was young. The role play allowed me to show a different side of myself that both of us enjoyed. We summon my inner hussy on a monthly basis now!"

—JULIA, 24, GRADUATE STUDENT

SEX TOYS

In a bit of unintelligent design, most sexual positions offer little clitoral stimulation, which women need to reach orgasm. Sex toys, then,
are accoutrement you can both get excited about. She may well be
using a vibrator when you're not around, so the main hurdle is
finding the stones to bring it up with her. "Men worry that they'll be
replaced, or that she'll become addicted and he'll never be able to
compete," says Johanson, who, by the way, is a 70-something registered nurse.

AT FIRST: Start with a bath and massage oils, suggests Mone. A
scientist named Tricia, 28, who admits to being uncomfortable with
non-traditional sex, says, "Even I'd be up for playing around with lu-
bricants and body butter." Then it's your move: Package some oils, a
toy, maybe some lingerie, and give it to her to peruse on her own
time. (Good Vibrations has a Friday Nite Delight kit with a bath ball,
orange-mango body oil, massage lotion, raspberry-chocolate-truffle
body butter, and a Magic Touch mini bullet vibrator; $35, good
vibes.com.) Tell her to bring her new toys along whenever she's ready.

LATER: The elusive simultaneous orgasm is more likely with the
right accessories. "If a woman uses a vibrator that sits on her clitoris,
she can climax while he's inside her," says Royalle. She recommends
the Natural Contours Superbe ($25, natural-contours.com), which,
though designed for mind-blowing sex, looks as sweet and innocent
as they come (ahem). When we took a group of nonkinky girls to
Good Vibrations, they were drawn to the smaller "ticklers." "They
didn't intimidate me as much as the dildo-y-looking stuff," says
Carley. And for men? They can work on you, too: "Once they get used
to the idea, guys love vibrators," says Johanson. "If she takes it and
rubs it up the shaft, over and around the head and testicles—that's
very stimulating." Lube helps.

HER STORY: "My guy is really great in bed, but I just couldn't
come through sex alone. I really wanted us to experience orgasm si-

multaneously. When my boyfriend surprised me with a vibrator that looked more like a lipstick, we finally experienced what we were looking for, and it was everything I thought it would be."

—MELISSA, 31, ACCOUNTANT

EXHIBITIONISM

We're talking all types: flashing, sex in a public place, sex in a private place with open drapes, wearing a skirt but no underwear. "The thrill of being viewed has a lot to do with getting attention," says Queen. "For women, it's a sort of centering experience that makes them realize they have attractiveness and erotic energy."

AT FIRST: Go commando when you leave the house, with her in a skirt or dress. Throughout the evening, give each other a few quick, private shows. Use any opportunity—helping her with a pool shot, pressing up against each other—to get all up in her business. "After a quickie, we were late meeting friends for drinks, and in the rush to get dressed, I decided to forgo my underwear," says Karen, a 25-year-old writer. "I'd be talking to my friends or ordering a drink, and he'd reach his hand up my skirt. It wouldn't have happened if the bar hadn't been dark and we hadn't been drunk, but I'm so glad I did it."

LATER: Sex outdoors. "The fear of getting caught really wakes you up and focuses you on the sexual experience," says Queen. "It also harks back to the thrill of sexual experiences as teenagers, when we had so little privacy." Be strategic, and keep an eye out for Johnny Law.

HER STORY: "It was the hottest thing ever. This guy asked me to join him for a bottle of wine on the roof of his apartment building. Before long, we were doing it standing up, my legs wrapped around him. I'm a shy person, but it brought out something in me. I'm the epitome of a law-abiding citizen. I think that made the vague threat of being caught all the more thrilling."

RACHEL, 29, SPEECH PATHOLOGIST

Take Her Home Tonight

Some women are looking to go wild for a night. Here's how to find them and make it happen

BY NICOLE BELAND

HERE'S WHAT I REMEMBER about the best one-night stand of my life: everything but his name. He was a bartender/actor who rode a beat-up motorcycle, but I didn't find that out until after his jeans came off. It started in a bar. He sat down next to my girl-friend and me—we were having a giggly girls' night out—stared in the other direction, and didn't say a word.

After 10 minutes, he asked if I would watch his stuff while he went outside to make a call. When he came back, he grimaced like De Niro and thanked me very politely. By that point, I was already curious about whom he had called, what was in his faded leather bag, and why he wouldn't smile. So I asked if he was having a bad day. Within a couple of hours, we were naked in bed together. And then he was gone.

To this day, I have to admire how smooth he was, because great one-night stands are tough to pull off. Plenty can go wrong between the first long look and the next-day e-mail. This is what you need to know to do it exactly right. You can thank me in the morning.

WHERE TO FIND HER

Weddings, for one. "Seeing two people completely in love, combined with an open bar, always gets my hormones raging," says my friend Katie, who admits to slipping out of her sister's wedding reception with a member of the catering staff. Other events and places that rev up the female libido include vacations, holidays, birthday bashes (especially our own), dance clubs, balmy summer nights, and disastrous incidents (personal or global) that inspire us to seize the moment as well as the nearest man.

DON'T LOOK HERE: Work events can buzz with sexual tension, but few women are willing to taint their professional reputations by giving the office something to snicker about. Dinner parties are too proper, and family get-togethers are out of the question. No girl thinks about sex when Uncle Nick's butt cracks a smile every time he reaches for a bocce ball.

HOW SHE ACTS

A girl with naked Twister on her mind is usually trying to be noticed. "If I want to hook up, I'll be at the bar, on the dance floor, and frequently circling the room trying to make eye contact with a hot guy," says my friend Sophie. Look for the women who are clearly out to have fun, who are laughing their butts off, who are dancing on the dirty side, and who keep glancing around the room to see who glances back. There's no guarantee that they're out to get laid, but there's no harm in introducing yourself and finding out.

WALK AWAY: That girl in the corner, sipping Shiraz? Not in the mood to make out with a stranger.

WHAT SHE WANTS

Women like to be pursued, but in the land of one-night stands, most of us prefer to play the seductress. It's our way of turning the stereotypical one-nighter paradigm on its head—taking "advantage" of the man for a change.

LET HER LEAD: Stow your witty pickup line. You're better off with something straightforward, like, "Hi, I'm Jeff." "A hookup is the one time a girl will judge a guy 95 percent by his looks," says Katie. But relax—that doesn't have to mean flawless looks: "A great smile and muscular shoulders can be very persuasive." Work your warm vibe and back it up with stylish (but not too slick) clothes, direct eye contact, and a clean, manly scent. Linger in her vicinity; respond when she flirts. But, for the first few stages, let her take the lead.

WHAT YOU WANT

If you want to call yourself a gentleman—and ward off any chance that your hookup will start phoning you 50 times a day—make this known: You're not looking for a girlfriend. "All a guy has to do is make it clear that he's far too busy for a relationship these days, or that he loves being single," says Sophie. "That way he eliminates any idea a girl might have that their one night of fun will lead to anything more substantial." No doubt the woman is perfectly aware of this, but it's better to be clear than to be called a bastard.

MANAGE EXPECTATIONS: Your declaration must happen long before your pants hit the floor. Otherwise, she might fall for you somewhere between the first kiss and the last thrust.

WHEN YOU KNOW

How can you tell if the game is on? It's when she suggests—or agrees with your suggestion—that you go to another bar (that quieter one down the road). Here's how the woman's mind is working, as explained by Katie: "It brings you one step closer to going home together, but provides a little buffer that makes the whole thing feel more in control."

SHUT UP AND KISS HER: Once you've reached the new, preferably dark and loungey locale, the first kiss is only a drink away. "I love it when a guy leans very close to me and pauses," says Sophie. "Then we both come in for the kiss." Thus begins a long and hot public display of affection, after which one of you will ask if you should go someplace private.

Respect Yourself in the Morning

Five Ethical Principles of Random Hookups

Enjoying a one-night stand doesn't make you a bad person—but treating your partner like a disposable sex toy does. "An 'ethical slut' is a person who celebrates sex with a variety of partners who, at the same time, has a respect for everyone's feelings and rights," says Dossie Easton, a marriage and family therapist and coauthor of *The Ethical Slut: A Guide to Infinite Sexual Possibilities*. Embrace her principles and remain a gentleman. Easy, right?

HONESTY. Don't lie to yourself, or to her. If you suspect that the woman isn't 100 percent comfortable with having sex, or if she's acting on a long-simmering crush while you just want some no-attachment fun, politely cut things short. "The best way to engender respect is by being willing to be honest, and that starts with being honest with yourself," says Easton.

RESPONSIBILITY. Nothing is more mood-bursting than a fling who grumbles about using protection.

HOW TO BEHAVE (OR NOT)

Your best bet is to go to her place, not yours. She'll feel more comfortable, and you'll have the option of splitting before dawn. Small talk is a buzz kill; compliments are okay. Tell her that she's beautiful and incredibly sexy, then let the kissing and undressing begin—as in the second you walk through the door. You're both in this for the sex, so make it adventurous.

JUST DO IT: Use a condom, of course, and no spanking, backdoor entry, kinky toys, or uncomfortable positions (unless she makes a specific request). Go with the standard stuff, plus plenty of enthusiastic squeezing, licking, sucking, stroking, rubbing, moaning, and maybe even a little pinching.

RESPECT. Lose this attitude: *I have many needs, and she's letting me take advantage of her.* "Sex is empowering and wonderful for everyone who partakes in it," Easton says. You're partners in this escapade.

POLITENESS. Both men and women often put up a tough veneer to compensate for the emotional disconnect of being intimate with a stranger. Engage in some postcoital pillow chatter; it's only polite. Be appreciative and complimentary. "Letting people know that you respect who they are makes them feel good about themselves and the night," says Easton.

CONSIDERATION. Easton calls a common scenario "the tyranny of hydraulics": "First this, then that, and it all ends when the guy comes." Try mixing up the sequence by performing oral sex after you've had intercourse—a move that ensures you'll leave a woman satisfied and makes you look like the unselfish, ethical slut you are.

WHEN TO LEAVE

Ask her straight out whether she wants you to stay or make yourself scarce.

TELL HER THE TRUTH: Tell her you had a great time. Don't say, "I'll call you" or "Maybe we can see each other again" if it isn't true. And if you want to earn a spot on her booty call list—or be the type of one-night wonder she might recommend to a friend—send her a single e-mail the next day saying that last night was amazing and she should feel free to contact you if she ever wants to "do it" again.

The Make-Out Manual

To generate serious romantic heat, remaster
the lost art of necking

BY NICOLE BELAND

SQUEAKING BACK AND FORTH on top of a half-deflated pool float in a backyard shed, my 15-year-old boyfriend and I were soaking wet and groping each other frantically. After dating for 5 months and making out in the deep end of my best friend's pool for 5 minutes, we decided: We were going all the way. Greg's trunks were already around his knees, but he'd been tugging so wildly on my wet bikini strings that they were tied into impossibly tight little knots. Just when he had the brilliant idea to push aside the damp strip of fabric between my legs, we heard giggling outside the shed door. The other party guests were on to us. As usual, we were left unfulfilled, blushing, and shaking with the kind of brain-melting horniness that seldom strikes past age 18.

Most of my teenage trysts were just as clumsy and ultimately frustrating, but they were unfailingly memorable. Looking back, there's more than one aspect of those underage experiences that I'm eager to relive. I long for a hot and horny encounter that's just as frantic but nowhere near as fumbling; just as unpredictable but a lot more pleasurable. At 30, what I want is a hormone-fueled high-school hookup with a fully grown man. I bet the woman in your life feels the same way. Use these instructions to treat your next date as if you were once again getting lucky in the back of your parents' sensible station wagon. It will be hot, I promise.

STEAL THE FIRST KISS

My friend Anna will never forget the time her 10th-grade crush grabbed her hand at a school dance and led her into a dimly lit hallway. "He didn't say a word, just pressed my body up against the lockers, and before I knew what was happening, he was sucking on my bottom lip," she remembers. "My knees wobbled for the rest of the night."

Ten years later, it's become standard behavior for Anna's dates to wait until the end of the night to politely lean toward her for a good-night peck. Boring. Remember that women of all ages want to be wanted—and I mean really wanted. Anna's advice: "Grab me around the waist and plant one on me, damn it." What's important is that you go after that first smooch with gusto—put some pressure into it, open your mouth a little—and do it at a daring, instead of glaringly obvious, moment. Kissing her in the middle of the date is what will deliver a thrill straight to the base of her spine. It's risky, yes, but the payoff is worth it.

SLIP INTO THE CLOSET

One night during junior year, my boyfriend and I managed to get kicked out of a pizza place, an arcade, and the parking lot behind the public library for what you might call "public indecency." Goaded by hormones that knew no limits, we weren't discouraged. We drove out of town and turned off at the first field we came to, heading straight into the waist-high grass, where we could finally grope each other in peace. Having no idea where or when we'd get our hands on one another was thrilling in itself. It made us spontaneous and brave. We were constantly on the lookout for empty closets, dark corners, and seldom-used stairwells.

Somewhere between then and now, most of us have stopped viewing any place but the bedroom as a viable hookup location, but those little nooks are still there, waiting to be used for all sorts of naughty purposes. All it takes is a quick nudge into the coat-check room and you and your date will be rocketing back to the Junior Ring Dance, circa 1989.

EXPLOIT HER SWEATER

For a woman, wearing a soft sweater without a bra is one of the great simple pleasures of life. The fabric gently gliding over bare breasts is cozy and erotic at the same time, and it made my high-school boyfriends crazy with desire to run their hands over my pink fuzzies.

Cuddly tops, flowing silk skirts, fishnet stockings: They all feel as good to our skin lying underneath as they do to your hands. And don't underestimate the thrill of pure, simple cotton. "Having soft cotton panties between my body and a man's fingers is absolute heaven," says Anna. Our most tender parts can be extremely sensitive, and sometimes indirect contact is even more pleasurable than skin-on-skin. As it was at the make-out party, so it is right now: Women still love to be felt up both above and below the belt. Slowly at first, with caressing fingers, and then with increasing pressure and plenty of that blessed thing called friction.

QUIT WHILE IT'S HOT

I remember the heart-thumping panic I felt when the clock on the dashboard revealed that it was 11:55 p.m., which meant I had less than 5 minutes to untangle myself from my date, reassemble my outfit, and hustle home before curfew. Having to stop cold when my body was at the height of arousal was painful—and I'm sure it hurt my boyfriend even more than it hurt me. But, oooh, did it hurt so good. It left us wanting . . . no, desperate, for more. The carryover horniness was the ultimate aphrodisiac.

And now, delayed gratification certainly still has its perks. Recently, when I decided to go home alone after a hot-and-heavy date that involved X-rated behavior in the back of a cab, I spent the next 3 days thinking of nothing but him. I dwelled on the memory of our chemistry and the imagination of what might happen next. It all became magnified in my mind until I was convinced that we had something special, something out of this world. And when that wish was fulfilled, guess what? We did.

Find Her Online

Make yourself irresistible on Internet dating sites without lying—
and get stunning results

BY LISA JONES

FIRST QUESTION: Are you single?

Second question: Are you online?

If yes to both, skip to where I tell you how to spend less time pecking away at your keyboard and more time getting some e-booty, or a meaningful relationship—whatever your goal is.

If yes to number one and no to number two—you're a single guy who's not looking online—let's chat. I know what you're thinking. When I put my L-search on broadband a few months ago, I felt very late to the party. And I thought I would hate it. But after giving it a go, I solemnly say: If you're offline, you're single, and you want to hook up, it's time to upload your kisser and your brand of smooth for the millions of ladies online to check out.

Be aware: The e-fishing pond is more competitive than ever. On most sites, men outnumber women. On match.com, the guy-girl ratio is 60:40. On others, it's worse: 70:30. That's why you need this guide. "Any guy who's complaining about being single, and who at this late date does not have an online profile as part of his diversified dating portfolio, should stop complaining," says Lynn Harris, a journalist who helps online daters perfect their profiles at personalstrainer.com. "Having a profile online is like having another credit card in your wallet; it's there as backup."

It's just another way to meet women. My brother (jokingly) calls his online pool of ladies his "stable." As in, "I have a few new ladies in my stable this week." I think you should start building one. I'll help.

1. SHOW GOOD FACE

Women don't respond to messages without photos. We're shallow. We're suspicious. We think you're ugly and have a wife. On match.com, profiles with photos get up to 10 times more responses than those without. Make sure the photo is taken up close and in focus—no sunglasses, no hats. Would it kill you to smile?

One man I went out with had a profile shot of himself at the wheel of a sailboat: superhot. Normally I don't recommend props, and normally I'd be suspicious of a show-off. But this worked.

What I won't respond to is a photo of a shirtless man—even if you're on the beach; even if you have *Men's Health* abs. It is never a good idea. In the female mind, hottest is the man who appears not to realize he's attractive. The shirtless man thinks he's hot, and that instantly makes him unhot.

2. GIVE GOOD WORD

It's like freshman comp:

SHOW, DON'T TELL. Saying you're funny has no meaning if nothing in your profile makes me laugh. Saying you're adventurous isn't nearly as interesting as describing your kite-boarding weekend.

DO A CLICHÉ CHECK. Even if you are a good listener who likes museums, sunsets, and walks in the park, don't say so. Cheese like this gave personals a bad name.

SPELLING COUNTS. Not because we're picky bitches. But when we see misspellings, we think, *How badly does this guy want to meet someone?* "Maybe that's not fair. But that's all we have to go on," says Harris, who is also the cocreator of breakupgirl.net.

3. RECRUIT A WINGWOMAN

My friend Matt (whom I used to date) sheepishly told me he had started online dating. Of course, I stalked him on nerve.com.

Yikes! The handsome face I know was in his photo—but he was holding a baby. (Bad move. It's cloying and makes a woman wonder whose baby it is.) And his answer to the question "What's your favorite on-screen sex scene?" involved gay porn. (It was a joke, but the humor didn't translate.) I called him; I advised him. He changed the answer; he changed the photo. He immediately received messages from five new women. (And that's the power of my advice, boys.)

Before going public, ask a lady friend (the kind you would like to date) to look at your profile. Or hire someone: At personals trainer.com, an expert can tune up your profile or write it for you.

4. CHOOSE THOUGHTFULLY

I have this theory about dating, and it's especially true online. When you go after a woman you're truly interested in—instead of just any random girl—you're more likely to get her. You come across as enthusiastic and genuine. When you first start e-dating, there's an eBay effect: You want everything you see.

But if you're writing generic messages to hundreds of women, they won't respond. "Women are actually quite sophisticated online daters today," says Trish McDermott, who was part of the founding team of match.com, where 15 million people are members. "They know when they're getting spammed—when a guy is just playing the numbers game."

5. MAKE ME CARE

Winks are for wusses. (It's a half-assed message that says my profile caught your eye.) I'm not so crazy about the IM option, either. Send me an actual e-mail. In the subject line, most guys write "Hi" or "Hey," so at least add my user name. Or write something like "Caring is creepy," because my profile says I like the *Garden State* soundtrack. Then I'll feel like you get me.

It doesn't matter much what you say in your message. Make a connection based on something you noticed in my profile. Say that of all the women you saw online, I'm the one who stood out. If you show genuine interest in me and I like what I see, you'll keep my attention, and I'll respond.

6. ASK ME OUT ALREADY

If we've e-mailed a few times, it's a safe bet to invite me out for coffee or a drink, or ask for my phone number. If you wait too long, I might lose interest or start building expectations. "Too many online exchanges and we start creating fantasy women and men in our minds," says McDermott, "and then they don't live up to the fantasy."

7. CALM MY FEARS

I'll assume you're a weirdo/psycho/probable rapist until you demonstrate otherwise. Don't be offended. Women still have safety concerns. Let me take the lead in revealing personal information, like where I live. Otherwise, once we're on a date and have exchanged last names, consider it regular dating, and work your magic, normal-style.

Very important: If you're just looking for sex, make sure you're targeting women who are clearly doing the same. On most sites, you can specify whether you're looking for play or intimate encounters, friendship, dating, or a serious relationship. E-mailing a woman who's in the serious-relationship category when you're listed in intimate encounters is a waste of time—and, really, it's rude and creepy. Shout-out to the guys who want to "play": No, I will not meet you on the No. 6 train. I will not meet you anywhere.

Down Girl! When She's Trying Too Hard

Sarah Miller answers tough questions about how to tone her down

What do I do when she says "I love you" too soon?

Don't say it back just to make the moment less awkward, because a year from now you could find yourself married, and that would be really awkward. Also, don't pretend you didn't hear her, because she will repeat it. Instead, say something like, "Wow, that means a lot to me, but I'm not quite there yet." If she gets mad, she's not worth it. And she may be insane.

What do I do if she wants me to meet the parents when I'm just not there yet?

You can put this off once and hope it doesn't come up again until you're good and ready. If it does, and you're still interested in her, go ahead and meet them. (You're not committing to anything, and at the very least, you'll get a free meal.) When you do, just be yourself, maybe minus the third drink and the f-word. The Boy Scout/salesman routine is transparent to her folks, not to mention exhausting for you. Show some but not too much interest in them. She'll be impressed by your social skills but not jealous that you're not paying enough attention to her.

She has a special ring tone on her cell phone for me!

If that special ring tone is "I Want to Hold Your Hand," run away quickly. Otherwise, make a point of always asking for her phone number when you talk. She'll get the hint that even if this relationship is in ink for her, it's still in pencil for you.

She constantly calls me at work.
We women are better multitaskers than men are, so it doesn't occur to us that you can't write a contract, eat a sandwich, and analyze a best friend's problems at the same time. This is a good one to blame on someone else: "The boss doesn't like us to get too many calls" works. Or, to look more like your own man: "I wish I could talk to you all day, but it's not very private here."

What do I do when she wants to know where I am every second of the day?
Start calling her literally every time you change venue and activity: "I'm heading out of the bathroom now." "Now I'm going into the elevator." "I'll call you as soon as I'm in the car . . . I'm turning on the radio now . . . driving now." If she doesn't think this is funny, dump her.

QUICKIES

Master the Gesture

Women like romance, but lots of men don't have the time or P. Diddy budget to follow through. Women worth pursuing see grandness in the kind of gesture that costs little beyond some consideration and imagination. Like these:

> "I had to clutch my winter coat around my neck because I lost a button on it. I had just met my husband-to-be, and he showed up on one of our dates with a button. It was a brilliant little gesture, and it only cost him about $2." —CARLA, 34

> "When I was sick, my boyfriend left a can of soup and a card on my doorstep. It was so sweet and simple." —MELISSA, 21

> "My date brought fresh strawberries. It was a clever switch from flowers, and you can enjoy the berries together."
> —CAROL, 30

> "When Adam finally let me wear his cherished Kirk Gibson jersey, I knew he was in love with me." —MARIA, 25

> "A guy gave me a pot of soil. He said he wanted to be around when the seeds in it sprouted—very romantic." —ELAINE, 28

Future Hotness

How can you tell what a woman will look like in 10, 20, or 30 years?
—P., HOLLYWOOD, FL

First, the obligatory tirade against shallowness: "Marry a girl because you love her, not based on how she looks," says Seth Matarasso, MD, a San Francisco dermatologist. "Because I'm telling you right now— looks fade." Okay, moving on. Ask yourself the following:

WHO'S HER DADDY? Check out Mom and Dad. "Look at the hair, the skin, the wrinkles," says Dr. Matarasso. "Do they have that turkey-wattle neck? Do their earlobes sag?" Genetic tags are the biggest indicators of future aging.

WHERE'S SHE FROM? If she grew up in beautiful Seattle, she'll be less leathery than if she was raised in Death Valley. Most sun damage happens in our childhood years, when we didn't have jobs to keep us indoors.

WHERE IS SHE NOW? "Is she living where the air is clear and there are no pollutants? Those have a direct effect on your skin," says Dr. Matarasso.

WHAT DOES SHE DO? High-stress jobs can add just as many years to a woman's face as to any man's. And if she works in a bar or another environment where she's exposed to secondhand smoke, it'll have the same drying, damaging effect as if she were a smoker herself.

PHEROMONES STINK

Is there any science backing up pheromones and how they attract women? Do pheromone supplements work? —R.E., PLANO, TX

Sorry, fellas, but a shower and a smile will go a lot farther with the ladies than your sweaty armpits will. The notion of sex-attracting pheromones was first propounded 50 years ago, when a scientist noticed that male moths stayed upwind to attract female moths with their scent. This is true for moths, but no such phenomenon has ever been shown to apply to humans, says Charles Wysocki, PhD, a neuroscientist at the Monell Chemical Senses Center in Philadelphia and author of the study "Facts, Fallacies, Fears and Frustrations with Human Pheromones." "There is no biomedical literature to support the claim that humans use attraction pheromones," he says. What about the supplements sold on the Internet? "Buyer beware," says Wysocki. "Their claims are anecdotal. There is no scientific proof that those products actually work."

CAN YOU MEET ME NOW?

Online dating is going wireless. A new application for cell phones will be able to tell you if a compatible woman is nearby. The software, Serendipity, is available free at mobule.net for Nokia phones, with other types of compatible phones to follow. Users submit profiles, and if the service senses a potential match nearby—someone who has also created a profile—it'll send photos to both users' phones so they can recognize each other. Nathan Eagle, a PhD candidate at MIT who developed the program, thinks it'll also be useful for meeting business contacts and friends of friends. And, yes, you can turn off your beacon anytime you want.

INSTANT SEXPERT

Facts of the Phone

Number of men (and women) who've used a text message to break up with someone: **1 in 5**

Number of men who've secretly checked the text messages in their partner's phone: **1 in 3**

What the average guy considers the worst moment for his cell phone to ring: **during sex**

Percentage of men who say they've used their cell phones to "drunk dial" an ex: **45**

ASK THE GIRL
NEXT DOOR
The honest truth about women
from our lovely neighbor

Work Release
Where have you met the men you've dated? —HENRY, SACRAMENTO, CA

At work or through work. Sure, I've met interesting, attractive men at
all sorts of venues—parties, bookstores, concerts—and have gone on
a date or two with them. But the boyfriends I've stuck with long term
were guys who worked in the same office (though in a different department) or whom I met through work-related events. In retrospect,
I clicked with them because we already had so much in common. So
don't skip the company picnic this year or that conference you may be
considering. You can often get busy under the guise of doing business.

Rebound and Score
**The woman of my dreams was taken—until yesterday. How long do
I wait before asking her out?** —ANONYMOUS

If what you're after is a meaningful relationship that could actually go
the distance, wait until she's clearly stopped sulking and is acting like
her upbeat self again. I'm thinking that'll be about 3 months.

    If it's a fling you're after, wait a couple of weeks, then just go for it.
She'll be eager for a distraction and secretly hoping that sex with a
new guy will help get the ex off her mind.

Hot or Not
**Are average-looking women more receptive to a man's come-on
than really attractive women are?** —MATTY, BILOXI, MS

Think you have a better chance with the not-so-cute girl? With the exception of fraternity parties, the answer is no. An average-looking

woman might be more flattered by the attention because she doesn't get it as often, but that doesn't mean she'll be any more eager to tear off her undies than a Cameron Diaz look-alike. Every woman's attitude toward being picked up is different. Some of the most gorgeous women I know will give any guy 10 minutes to prove his worth, while some less conventional beauties wouldn't give a stranger the time of day.

Last (Booty) Call

I was dating a woman and things were going well—until she dumped me after we had sex for the second time. Was it because of the sex? —G.W., ST. PAUL, MN

Without knowing anything else about the relationship or the sex: maybe. If you did something odd or offensive—like wiggling a finger in her ear while ecstatically rubbing the outside of your chinos or "accidentally" inserting your member somewhere other than the preferred female orifice—then yes, it was the sex. More likely, she already had her hand on the chain, and a night of lame booty was all she needed to pull the plug. Women don't usually expect fantastic sex on the first, second, or even third attempt. We figure it takes time to relax and get used to each other. Plus, we have a habit of blaming ourselves when sparks don't fly between the sheets.

SEX MATTERS

Sex may not be the only thing that keeps a relationship together, but it's mighty important. Expressing your love and affection for your partner through slow, meaningful, attentive sex is one of the best ways to bond. But don't be fooled. You don't always have to be a Casanova between the sheets. One of the biggest misconceptions is that women always expect all-night, candlelit, tantric sex à la Sting and Trudie Styler. Not true. In fact, there are times when women are more than willing to partake in a wild tryst, complete with unabashed screams and moans, or a quickie that will leave both of you panting and satisfied. Keeping your lovemaking style fresh and varied is the real key.

In the following pages, you'll discover the safest (and not so safe) places to do the deed, find where you stand on the sex-know-how scale, and learn how to satisfy your lover enough to keep her coming back for more.

Where the Sex Is Dirty

Some cities are filthy with roaches. Others are infested with bed bugs—the kind you get through unprotected sex. In fact, if it were possible to put Detroit beneath a microscope, you'd see that it's literally crawling with the critters. The Motor City is now the easiest place for an STD to hitch a ride.

How do we know? We collected the next best thing to block-by-block blood samples: the most recent rates of gonorrhea, syphilis, and chlamydia, as reported to the Centers for Disease Control and Prevention (CDC). And for those cities that aren't required to kiss and tell their STD rates to the CDC, we examined county data, from which we also pulled the most current HIV mortality rates. After analyzing all of these highly infectious numbers in our statistical petri dish, we were able to name the cities most likely to make love hurt—and those where sex is still just good clean fun.

Top 10—Good Clean Fun

1. Anaheim, CA ....A+

2. Santa Ana, CA ....A+

3. Spokane, WA ....A+

4. Modesto, CA ....A

5. **Madison, WI** ....A

6. Plano, TX ....A

7. Lincoln, NE ....A

8. Riverside, CA...............................A

9. San Jose, CA ....A

10. Akron, OH...A-

Bottom 10—Love Hurts

1. Chicago, IL ....F

2. Richmond, VA ....F

3. New Orleans, LA...........................F

4. Memphis, TN ....F

5. Philadelphia, PA...............................F

6. Washington, DC ....F

7. Atlanta, GA ....F

8. Baltimore, MD...........................F

9. Newark, NJ...............................F

10. Detroit, MI ....F

Bring Out Her Wild Side

Your fantasy woman—a reckless babe with a lustful mind—just might be the one you're with. Here's how to set her loose

BY LIESA GOINS

YOUR CLASSY LADY might just be a naughty superfreak on the inside—it's up to you to coax that out of her. The key: Tell her it's okay. "Women are conditioned to fulfill the role of 'good girl,'" says Judith Sherven, PhD, coauthor of *Be Loved for Who You Really Are*. "They need permission from you to break that mold, to change from being their parents' good girl to being your hot girlfriend." Here's how.

GIVE HER THE POWER. Imagine her doing something wild, then describe it to her. "You have to see her that way before she'll be able to act that way," says Sherven. "She has to feel confident that you think she's capable of it."

SHOW HER OFF. "In public, whisper how much she turns you on, and combine that with some neck kissing," says Ian Kerner, PhD, author of *She Comes First*. Get her used to feeling sexy in public and she'll reciprocate in private.

GRANT HER WISHES. If she's joked about skinny-dipping, find a lake. If she's mentioned skydiving, book the plane. "Overcoming her fears with her will build trust and make her more likely to go out on a limb the next time," says Yvonne Fulbright, author of *The Hot Guide to Safer Sex*. You're giving her the security to be daring.

TEASE HER ALL DAY. Plant a long kiss on her in the a.m. and tell her you can't wait to ravage her later. "Knowing you find her irresistible is the ultimate turn-on," says Regena Thomashauer, author of *Mama Gena's Marriage Manual*. Follow up with phone calls and you'll both be counting the hours.

How Can You Resist?

When she offers forbidden pleasures, it's tempting to forget your vows. Before you go any closer, read this

CAROLINE TIGER

YOU'VE MET HER, maybe you work with her—the woman who hints at possibilities. But when flirting turns to invitation, and it's definitely not your imagination, you have a decision to make. Will you exit gracefully or act disgracefully?

"Rather than say, 'I would never have an affair,' be honest and look at what makes you vulnerable," says Barry McCarthy, PhD, coauthor of *Getting It Right the First Time: Creating a Healthy Marriage.* As in driving, it's easier to avoid dangerous situations than escape from them. Here's your road map.

THE CHUMMY COWORKER

ASK YOURSELF: Am I treating her just as I would a male coworker? "If not, then that's your warning," says Don-David Lusterman, PhD, a couples therapist and the author of *Infidelity: A Survival Guide.* "Reestablish a formal relationship and call her Ms. Cooper, not Debra."

WHEN YOU'RE TOGETHER: "Never close your door or blinds," says Scott Haltzman, MD, creator of the site SecretsofMarriedMen.com. "The more eyes on you, the better." Never gripe about your home life—it's an invitation for her to "demonstrate she's better than what you have," he says.

THE STILL-HOT EX

ASK YOURSELF: Could my wife (or girlfriend) be invited to this rendezvous? If not, "don't have that meeting with the ex," Dr. Haltzman says. "You need to remind yourself of how this woman was bad for you. Repeat the mantra: 'She's trouble—run.'"

WHEN YOU GO: Tell your wife you're going to see the ex. "This automatically helps keep you in line because you know that when you get home, your wife is going to ask you about it," Lusterman says.

THE BIZ-TRIP TEMPTRESS

ASK YOURSELF: What will happen after the sex? "The more you think it through, the easier it is to walk away," Lusterman says. Imagine everyone you're near has a hotline to your wife, Dr. Haltzman suggests. Then imagine her look of horror and despair.

WHEN SHE KEEPS TOUCHING YOUR FOREARM: Blurt out, "I'm married" or "I have a girlfriend." "It's to remind yourself of your situation as much as it is to inform her," says Judith Sherven, PhD, coauthor of *Be Loved for Who You Really Are*. And have a "trouble buddy" stand by to bust you if you start canoodling.

WHEN YOU FEEL THE URGE: "Go to a bathroom and masturbate," says Ian Kerner, PhD, a clinical sexologist and the author of *She Comes First*. "This can relieve some sexual tension and give you about 30 minutes of sanity. Use this window to get out of Dodge."

Be Her Best Ever

The *Men's Health* Orgasm Guide: Five new ways to play
BY IAN KERNER, PHD

Until a few years ago, my sex life was like an endless TiVo loop of *Lost*. I wasn't sure where I was or what I should do, and there were startling noises in the dark. For my girlfriends, each episode was frustrating—all tease, no climax.

Today I'm off the island, relieved and happy. I have a PhD in clinical sexology, which is a fancy way of saying I've done my share of analysis and have, I think, deciphered the code of female sexual satisfaction.

In short, I've figured out what the heck is going on. It's mostly a matter of tuning in to her body and needs. Here's a synopsis, including the "tools" needed to find your way out of the wilderness and lead her to happiness.

TECHNIQUE: ROPE-A-DOPE

FOR: Clitoral Stimulation

TOOL: Tongue

This is named after Muhammad Ali's strategy for toppling George Foreman. Ali stood there for seven rounds before springing to life and sending the tired Foreman to the mat. When it comes to cunnilingus, be like Ali.

- Conserve your energy, letting her do most of the work as she grinds on your tongue. Start with slow, rhythmic tongue strokes. Try a long, easy ice-cream lick from bottom to top that

covers the full span of her inner labia and ends with her clitoral head. No matter how worked up she becomes, keep it
slow and easy and consistent. Tease her into delirium, then . . .

- Hit her with a series of fast vertical and diagonal tongue
  strokes on her clitoris. Then . . .
- Return to slow, easy strokes.
- Repeat until she's out cold.

WHY IT WORKS: This method eases her gently into clitoral stimulation. The clitoris is extremely sensitive at the outset. You'll start her
blood flowing while offering the consistent stimulation she needs.
The bursts of vigor add surprise, spike her sexual response, and keep
her moving toward orgasm.

TECHNIQUE: HEART OF PALM

FOR: Clitoral stimulation, with optional G-spot stimulation
TOOLS: Your hands
Women never forget a nice pair of hands. Make yours memorable.

- Rest on your side. You have all night.
- Place your hand over her vulva, pressing on her pubic mound
  with the base of your palm. Let your fingers drape against
  her entire vulva.
- Let her push against your palm, and use your index and
  middle fingers to make rhythmic come-hither gestures along
  her vaginal entrance.
- Lightly stimulate her clitoral head with your fingertips.
  Gently pinch her labia.
- For variety, insert two fingers, pressing them up against the
  front wall of her vagina, simultaneously stimulating her clitoris and G-spot.

Why It Works: This stimulates her entire vulva, the location of
nerve endings that are often ignored. While she's pushing her clitoris
into your palm, you're free to do some fancy finger-work.

TECHNIQUE: HEAD-TO-HEAD

FOR: Clitoral stimulation

TOOL: Penis

Think of your penis as one of many tools in your sexual survival kit—not your only weapon. And remember to use it outside her vagina occasionally.

- Focus on shallow thrusts. In the missionary position, barely penetrate her vagina. Let your penis rest just inside her.
- Linger. Loiter. Meander. Press the head of your penis against her clitoral head. Or press the shaft of your penis against her clitoris and gently thrust between the folds of her labia without entering her.
- When you penetrate deeply, press your pelvic bone against her clitoris and hold the position.

WHY IT WORKS: You're hitting hot spots. Many of the nerve endings that contribute to orgasm are on the surface of her vulva and within the first inch or so of her vaginal entrance. When you penetrate deeply and hold, the sense of closeness combined with the clitoral sensation will overwhelm her.

TECHNIQUE: UPWARD AND ONWARD

FOR: G-spot stimulation

TOOLS: Hands, vibrator, penis

Her G-spot, which is the diameter of a dime, is on the front wall of her vagina, a few inches in. You can feel it swell during arousal. Think of it as more of an area than a spot. It responds to firmer pressure than the clitoris does, so your fingers or a vibrator will sometimes work better than your penis.

- Place an inch or two of a vibrator insider her vagina, then lift the vibrator to press her G-spot. Bring her legs together around the vibrator and stimulate her clitoris with your tongue.

• During intercourse, stimulate her G-spot by entering her from behind and pressing down on it. Use one hand to massage her pubic mound, which will stimulate her G-spot from the outside.

WHY IT WORKS: G-spot orgasms don't happen independently of clitoral orgasms. New research suggests that the spot may be the root of the clitoris. Always try to combine clitoral and G-spot stimulation, or at least alternate regularly.

TECHNIQUE: THE MULTIPLE WARHEAD

FOR: Multiple orgasms

TOOLS: Tongue, hand, penis, vibrator, patience

The best time to prove the phrase "There's more to sex than just orgasm" is after she's had one. (You are so damn understanding!) Women can have multiple orgasms because they retain blood in the pelvic area after orgasm. Her clitoris just needs a bit of recovery time because it becomes overly sensitive after orgasm.

• Return to foreplay. Focus on gentle full-body stimulation, then . . .

• Gradually introduce clitoral stimulation. Use a hand to gently tease her vulva—you can use a fingertip to trace the perimeter of her inner labia, or let her press into your palm and take the lead.

AND FINALLY: Remember to end on a high note. To paraphrase the pioneering sexologist Theodoor H. Van de Velde, it's in the moments after orgasm that a man proves if he's an "erotically civilized" adult. Translation: Don't forget to cuddle.

The Man's Guide Self-Test: Are You Lousy in Bed?

Sure, she says she's satisfied—now find out how she really feels

1. When does foreplay start?
A. When our lips first touch.
B. When I buy her a pint of beer.
C. When her shirt comes off.

Women like foreplay to stretch as far back as the first encounter of the night. "Great foreplay happens when you pay great attention," says Lou Paget, author of *The Great Lover Playbook*, "whether that means a neck massage or buying her something she likes, like her favorite drink." Once in the bedroom, undress her as slowly as possible.

2. Which animal is she most like during sex?
A. A monkey—inquisitive, playful.
B. A tigress—on the hunt, aggressive.
C. A trapped rabbit.

The sizzle fades when men always take the lead, says Linda De Villers, PhD, a sex therapist and the author of *Love Skills*. To break the rut, spend the evening flirting with her instead of making the first move. "Draw her into the dance," De Villers says. If she jumps you, she's bound to be a more enthusiastic bedmate and respect your seduction skills.

3. What do you touch to drive her wild?
A. Yourself.
B. Her clitoris.
C. The skin between her fingers.

Women are loaded with pleasure points. Use the unexpected ones to turn her on the most, says Ava Cadell, PhD, a sexologist and the author of *The Pocket Idiot's Guide to Oral Sex*. "We have erogenous zones all over our bodies." Explore and discover: Caress her navel, her inner thighs, between her toes, under her chin, and along her spine.

4. She digs what you're doing, so you . . .
A. Stay the course.
B. Do it faster and harder.
C. Find something else she likes.

Too often, men take a positive reaction as a cue to increase speed or intensity during penetration or oral sex. "If she says, 'That's wonderful,' keep doing it just the same," De Villers says. "Speeding up will overwhelm and numb her." If you must switch, slow down and don't go as deep, to stimulate the nerve endings in the front third of her vagina.

5. How thick is your position playbook?
A. I've worn out my copy of the Kama Sutra.
B. I'm a missionary man.
C. I like classics, with some experimentation.

Adventure is good, but only if you're both able and willing. "Take your cue from the woman," De Villers says. A position that's exciting for you may be a nightmare for her if she's self-conscious about her body or not strong or flexible enough to sustain it. Go for positions that allow her to be readily stimulated, like sitting in a chair or lying with her on top.

6. She's happiest . . .
A. In the morning—she glows.
B. In the early evening, before sex.
C. Right after sex.

"You can judge how you performed the night before by how she wakes up in the morning," Paget says. Satisfaction doesn't have to mean orgasm; for women, intimacy is just as important. But exhaustion can sometimes cloud her true emotions at night. If she draws you close to her in bed in the morning and sighs, that means she was fulfilled.

7. To impress a woman in bed, you . . .
A. Take off her bra with one hand.
B. Compliment every part of her body.
C. Show her why you're called "the Mouth."

"For a woman, sex starts between the ears and goes between the legs," Cadell says. Be vocal about how her body inspires you—you'll make her feel at home sans clothes and whet her appetite. If you pride yourself on one skill, such as oral sex, remember that not every woman loves it. You could be overselling yourself.

8. Sex sounds like . . .
A. *SportsCenter.*
B. Heavy breathing.
C. She's speaking in tongues.

"If she used to be talkative but suddenly clams up, you have a real problem," says De Villers. Get her talking about what she likes and what she's thinking. Avoid distractions, like the TV—they tell her you don't really care, which is a big mistake: "You're psychologically disconnected, and that can really destroy the experience for a woman."

SCORING

1. A = 2 points   B = 3 points   C = 1 point
2. A = 2 points   B = 3 points   C = 1 point
3. A = 1 point   B = 2 points   C = 3 points
4. A = 3 points   B = 1 points   C = 2 points
5. A = 1 point   B = 2 points   C = 3 points
6. A = 3 points   B = 1 point   C = 2 points
7. A = 1 point   B = 3 points   C = 2 points
8. A = 1 point   B = 2 points   C = 3 points

18 TO 24 POINTS: So you're the guy who's giving us all a bad name.
11 TO 17 POINTS: Tune in and take your time—she'll thank you.
10 POINTS OR LESS: Luckily, practice makes perfect, so get crackin'.

The Six Stages of Sex

A man's life is defined by the women who inhabit it.
Some will be angels. Some will be devils. And some will be
a little of both

BY THOMAS BELLER

1. AWAKENING

You see her all the time and she means nothing to you, but then one day you ring your best friend's front door and she pulls it open wearing panties and a v-neck t-shirt. All of a sudden your friend's older sister is the most important person in the world. You stand there rocking back and forth at eye level with about an acre of cleavage—it's a word you've never even heard before, but now its meaning, purpose, and consequence you comprehend completely.

She lets you in without a second thought. You don't count. You're only 11. So she thinks nothing of wandering around her little brother's room in panties and a frayed T-shirt pondering the mysteries of her life and babbling absentmindedly to her Little League audience.

There she sits pouting at her desk, staring down at a textbook. When you ask what she's studying, she brushes you off with "You wouldn't understand," followed by a more confiding "Ninth grade is really hard."

When she is not around, your friend regales you with tales of her outrageous behavior with her boyfriends. Either this girl, Betty—long, red hair framing a pretty, pale face; small feet with toenails painted bubble-gum pink—is a nymphomaniac, or her little brother has a feverish imagination.

Looking back at these tales, it almost sounds as if your friend is simply channeling pornography and projecting it onto his older sister. But it's not likely that he had seen much porn at 11, and furthermore, it was 1976. Porn was just being invented. There wasn't cable, really; no videotapes or DVDs, and certainly no Internet.

At the time, however, reality doesn't even matter. Your imagination has been primed. The girl herself is often inches away from you. You are in love, but you don't exist. She gazes out the window with a faraway look, while you stare at the promised land—her cleavage. Its geography occupies so much psychic space in your head that when in its actual presence, you feel as though you could at any moment dive into it and simply disappear.

Instead it is Betty who disappears; her mother has declared that it is no longer appropriate for her to share a bedroom with her younger brother and her younger brother's horny little friends, and so the house is rearranged, and Betty disappears behind a closed door, only to be seen fleetingly stomping out of the house in frayed jeans and clogs, on the way, no doubt, to a date who will treat her badly.

2. TORTURE

You are struggling with the concept of niceness and sex. Rationally, being nice should lead you toward the promised land of sex. But looking around, it seems that a lot of jerks are getting girls, and you, who try to be nice, are not. The concept that girls may actually be attracted to guys who are callous, blasé, and inconsiderate is very hard to comprehend.

The problem here is that there is this woman you are interested in, and you have made the mistake of making friends with her. You talk on the phone. You hang out together. She has you over to her house. There is a Jacuzzi in the back. Right there in the middle of the city, her parents, rich as Croesus, have installed a Jacuzzi. She invited you over; she invites you in. You emerge steaming and lie together wetly on towels draped over her bed. At this moment, you are acutely aware of the peachlike cleft at the tight spot where the bathing suit wraps between her legs. So tight, and yet there is a separation, and this separation is an invitation: Come on in! But you do not.

This is because you are a coward and a fool, but in fairness, the mistake was made some time ago. You went into the wrong room. The room had a label on the door that read "Friend." In this room, you will be separated by only a wall from another room called "Screwing, sucking, groaning, owning," and some other stuff. But you can no more walk though this wall than you can walk on water. You can just hear the noises. By which I mean she will tell you about that other room. So close, and yet so far. It's total torture.

There are instances when the wall melts. Later in life, you see examples of the wall just vanishing, and people say, "Oh, we were friends for years, and then one day we just looked at each other and . . . "

Sometimes the wall will simply vanish, and the prisoner of friendship is suddenly free to walk into that other room (whereupon he promptly becomes the prisoner of sex, but that is another matter). The problem is, the wall rarely disappears while your ear is pressed up against it.

3. SALVATION

The task of saving you from the hell of sexless adolescence is so great, it requires nothing less than an angel. You meet her at a club. The conversation moves quickly to kissing—familiar territory. Then she puts your index finger in her mouth and sucks it while looking you in the eye. Unfamiliar territory!

It happens, people do it, and, she tells you, you can be one of the people who do it. With her. Right now! She is an angel, this woman who says these magic words: "Here it is. You can have it." And so a whole new problem in life presents itself: What to do when you get what you want? This riddle will never be completely resolved, but your skill in finessing it will improve dramatically over time. Now, however, you are a beginner and clueless. You are in a car, or on a couch in the living room, or maybe in a basement rec room. Someone's parents are not home . . . but they might come home! So keep your ears tuned for the sound of a turning lock! Meanwhile, the angel is sitting next to you, spreading her wings figuratively or literally. And you . . . you choke. You freeze. A stern morality previously unknown to you suddenly rises up, and you wonder if this is the right thing to do. In no time at all, you are moonwalking out of that situation faster than Michael Jackson.

And a new place of shame is born—I mean a physical location that will never be the same again. Many a nook and cranny of our ancestral homes holds a reproach to your grown-up self! You might even point them out to friends later on as souvenirs of a more innocent time. "That's where Shelly Liebling was ready to do it," you say, "but I was, like, not ready to close the deal. Kind of sad, really."

But there will always be rec rooms and parents out for an evening; and one day, opportunity will knock once again. Bang, bang!

4. DAMAGE

You will, in the course of your adventures in love, get completely stomped on at least once. Ideally, this doesn't happen too soon, the serious stomping. Early on, it's best if there is at least a tiny bit of farce attached to your pain. Such as when your girlfriend who went to another college announces on your first Thanksgiving break that— surprise, surprise—she is seeing someone else. If you are lucky, the "someone else" will be a totally anonymous jerk-off without any famous relatives. If you are unlucky, your brand-new ex-girlfriend will be getting it from one of Norman Mailer's multitudinous spawn, and you will return to the campus library to discover that Norman Mailer has written every single volume in the school library, and they are all laughing at you.

The more serious stomping will come later, when a new element is added to the equation: blame. The blame is on you. You will have some woman, you will be into it, you will be into her, and she will just . . . be there. A fixture in your life. And then one day, the fixture will look at you with the exasperated look on her face, and you suddenly realize she has been wearing this look for a little while now. And you realize: "It's too late! You blew it!" And the fierce comeback attempt, the reformed you, the attentive you, the caring-and-loving you who is not too drunk at midnight, will in the end not be enough. At which point you may resort to slightly stalkerlike behavior, like encamping beneath her window. Eventually you will get the satisfaction you are looking for and see her with another man. Thus scalded, you finally begin to look elsewhere.

5. EXPERIENCE

Some women will have more than you. More money, more property, more scars (psychic and otherwise), more confidence, more experience in love, life, more years. It is in the company of an older woman, however, that you discover an asset you never realized you had. That asset is you. You and the thing in your pants. She has a lot of things: a house, a car, and, who knows, kids. She has things and a body that is perhaps just a little overripe, which, to some tastes, is perfect. You, on the other hand, have nothing. But there you are in her big house, in her big bed, making use of your most valuable asset: you! She has knowledge. You have energy. It's a very good combination. For the first time, your youth is an asset.

A slight aura of heroism suddenly surrounds you. Because you are rescuing her, somehow. You are rescuing her from her obnoxious husband (who probably never satisfied her anyway). You are the man. And at very little cost, at first. After a while, if you fall in love with an older woman, a problem develops—you want to catch up. You want somehow to join her in life, but she is further along than you, and she always will be. What you are really holding on to is that feeling of want, that hook of desperate need that you have for her to need you, and your asset.

6. LOVE

The aphrodisiac of wanting is well known. Want implies a desire for something not in your grasp. Wanting leads to getting. But from getting, we arrive at having, and this is another ball game.

And what about being in love with the woman who is in love with you? This creature is someone you want to sleep with and someone you want to talk to, and you can either take her out into the world and stand with her, or you can not take her out and just stand in your bedroom in your underwear. Maybe you get on the bed and jump up and down. Because, though you are a fool, you are her fool. She is the one you love, but she is also the one who—and this is certainly one of the most terrifying conditions a man can find himself in—loves you. One day your gaze wanders over the vast ocean of beautiful women walking around and fixes on one woman. A flicker of the animal, something rustles inside you. And then the predicament. To go forth or to stay where you are, with the one you have— she who loves you—and with whom, in spite of that, you still want to do the nasty. Often. You can go forth. But if you do, you can't ever come back. It's one or the other, either/or, this or that. And what is "that"? That is the endless ocean of possibility. And "this"? What is "this"? This is your life. Do you want to start living it?

One day you will say, I do.

QUICKIES

WHAT SHE'S THINKING

Show your lover this: Men's sexual fantasies focus on the desire and pleasure of their partners more than women's fantasies do, according to a University of California, Santa Cruz, study. It's not that we're so thoughtful and women are selfish (okay, maybe). It might have to do with what we're not getting in real life. Our desires may include receiving "clear and unambiguous indications" that a woman "desires and enjoys sex" with us, says study author Eileen Zurbriggen, PhD. A typical woman's "unmet need is for her own desire and pleasure to be given priority." Tell her your fantasy is to please her, and it's a win-win situation.

WHEN BOOTY CALLS . . .

Women generally don't tell us what they want in bed. Mostly, we men have to translate moans and read thoughts. "Images of women in media, lack of sex ed, and general cultural stigma can make women uncomfortable expressing what they want sexually," says Niels Teunis, PhD, an assistant professor of human-sexuality studies at San Francisco State University. And some women think giving a guy guidance will insult him. Until you convince her otherwise, pay attention to . . .

HER EYES. Holding eye contact is a sign of connection. If she turns away, it often means "try something else," says Erica Neuman, MS, a sexuality educator at MyPleasure.com. Except when she's near orgasm—then closed eyes mean good work.

HER HANDS. "If I'm experiencing something I don't want to end, I touch him with more pressure," says Tina, 24. "I'm not going to react to someone passionately if I don't like what's going on." Look for her to grab, push, or scratch you if you're doing something right. Then try to remember what you did.

HER IMAGINATION. Women sometimes feel that they have to create a persona to have sex, because it can be a safer way to communicate sexually, Neuman says. Encourage her to play a role (try your Colin Farrell accent) and she may feel freer to show or tell you what she wants. Or see if she's game for porn. (Stress that it's for her pleasure.) While watching, she can offer pointers about what excites her.

HER INITIATIVE. Notice what she does to you to turn you on. "I'll never touch or kiss or do anything to a guy that I wouldn't like done to me," says Rosie, 32. "So if I'm biting his neck or licking his nipple, that would excite me, too."

Pregnancy Tests

Most home pregnancy tests aren't reliable on the first day after a missed period, say University of New Mexico researchers. Only First Response Early Result detected 95 percent of pregnancies on the first day.

Bulges in Your Genes

What determines a man's individual sexual tastes, fantasies, and fetishes? In other words, why do I like women's feet so much?
—C.W., READING, PA

It ain't the shoes, C.W. It's worse: your mom and dad (cue agonizing Oedipal wail). "Men have fairly straightforward desires," says Michael Bader, PhD, author of *Arousal: The Secret Logic of Sexual Fantasies.* "The problem is that the mind is wired such that these desires are inhibited by feelings we all have, like guilt, shame, rejection, inferiority, and so on." Your parents influenced the development of these feelings. Some interpretations:

• **YOU LIKE DOMINANT WOMEN.** If Mom was emotionally distant or depressed, you may have grown up seeing women as too fragile to handle the actual level of your desire, so you fantasize about situations that put women in control.

• **YOU PURSUE YOUNGER WOMEN.** You may fear not being able to please more experienced women, since a younger partner is more receptive to what her "teacher" can deliver. Or maybe she's just really hot.

• **YOU CRAVE A THREESOME.** You may feel insecure. Being able to please two women signifies studliness.

• **YOU HAVE A FETISH.** You're afraid of being rebuked, so you focus arousal on an object or body part that won't call you a weirdo. As for the foot thing, Bader says these desires can be linked to a childhood pleasure. Tickling the cute babysitter's feet, perhaps?

Candle Power

My girlfriend has a hot body but won't have sex with the lights on. How can I make her loosen up? —M.S., PHILADELPHIA, PA

Doing it in the dark allows a woman to forget about body-image hang-ups (we've got plenty) and just have fun. You could help her—not "make her"—loosen up by reassuring her that you're attracted to every part of her body, exactly the way it is. Tell her that her thighs are gorgeous, that her butt is clearly the work of a higher being. Then slowly brighten things (one candle, then two), telling her how much it turns you on to see her during sex. It may sound silly, but the result—watching her grinding away in broad daylight—will be well worth it.

Quickie Thinking

How can I make my wife more interested in quickies?
—D.M., VIA E-MAIL

The reason most women shy away from a fast shag is because it's difficult for us to become aroused, aka wet, without a good deal of foreplay. Having sex under dry conditions isn't just unpleasant, it's painful. The solution: Make her slicker quicker. Oral sex is an excellent way to do that while simultaneously turning her on. The other great option is always having personal lubricant on hand. Consider carrying a single-use packet of lube in your wallet for impromptu seductions—lube-covered fingers can also help jump-start our libidos. My favorite nonsticky, superconcentrated brand is Pjur Woman Bodyglide (Pjur USA.com). A few drops is all it takes.

Bare Down There

Do you see this Brazilian bikini-wax trend lasting? I like the natural look. —MARC, NEW YORK, NY

The craze is waning, thank goodness. It was a painful, pointless trend that left women feeling frumpy if we had more than a guitar-pick-size patch of hair down there. Several of my fashion-forward friends say they now favor trimming off a little at the edges for neatness but leaving the rest alone. That sounds good—natural and low maintenance. But who can predict? Such is the nature of pointless trends.

Fire Down Below

How can I make a woman believe I really do like going down on her?
—ANTHONY, VIA E-MAIL

A woman's relationship with her vagina is a lot like your relationship with the engine of your car. We check the oil, we take it to the garage, we keep it clean and running smoothly. The idea of licking it—and enjoying licking it—strikes us as somewhere between ridiculous and gross. (Of course, most of us really love it when you do.) You need to remind her that you think of her vagina in a completely different and far more fascinating way. This means you can't just tell her that you "really do like going down on her"; you have to go nuts over it. Declare her vulva to be the most beautiful thing you've ever seen. Tell her you love how she tastes. Say it turns you on, and then show her the undeniably hard evidence. And, of course, the more often and enthusiastically you do it, the more obvious it'll be that, to you, mowing her lawn is anything but a chore.

IN FOR THE LONG HAUL

Chances are, upon entering coupledom, you're still in the "honeymoon" stage of your relationship. Things are just dandy. You still make each other laugh. You keep learning new things about one another. The sex is great. Everything still feels pretty exciting. But don't be fooled. This honeymoon high won't last forever. And one of the most important things to realize is that your relationship will continue to change throughout its duration. Eventually, it will require work. But it's a good kind of work. Believe us!

The benefits of being one half of a couple far outweigh those of being single. The evidence is in the chapter that follows. Not only will you find out how a relationship can positively affect your health, you'll learn how to keep it hot and how to pull the plug when it's not.

Spying in the Bedroom

Couples spend much of their time together unconscious. Here's a glimpse under the covers at **six** slumber-related stats, based on a Tylenol PM/Harris Interactive phone survey of 1,000 Americans

BY LISA JONES

1. Forty-seven percent say their partner snores at least sometimes.

2. Forty-one percent say they always resolve an argument with their spouse or partner before going to bed.

3. Ten percent sleep naked.

4. Fifty-eight percent of married people fall asleep within 20 minutes, compared with forty-four percent of single people.

5. Twenty-three percent say they'd dump a new lover who snored loudly.

6. Forty-seven percent say they'd tell a partner about a romantic dream involving one of the partner's friends or colleagues.

Current Affairs

Are you a one-woman man or a two-timing dog?

MATT MARION

O**DDS THE AVERAGE-GUY-AS-TEEN** cheated on his high-school sweetheart: **1 IN 7**

Number of men who are still cheating on girlfriends today: **1 IN 6**

Number who cheat on their wives: **1 IN 2**

The average adulterer's top trysting spots:

1. Her place

2. Cheap motel

3. Expensive hotel

Number of men who would feel justified in having an affair if their wives had one first: **2 IN 5**

Number of wives stepping out right now: **1 IN 4**

Number of wives who were two-timing back in 1991: **1 IN 10**

Percentage of the average detective's caseload devoted to catching unfaithful spouses: **70**

What the average guy would do if he walked in on his wife and another man: **WALK OUT AND FILE FOR DIVORCE**

Runner-up: **BEAT THE GUY TO A PULP**

What the average guy would do if he walked in on his wife in bed with another woman: **TRY TO INITIATE A THREESOME**

Number of men who say it wouldn't be cheating if they had sex with a clone of their wives: **2 IN 5**

Number of men who say visiting a strip club is cheating: **1 IN 2**

Of guys who visit strip clubs, the percentage who will buy at least one lap dance: **80**

Percentage of married women who say it's cheating to . . .

Romantically kiss another woman: **75**

Hold a woman's hand: **43**

Flirt: **38**

How much likelier the average guy is to accidentally get his mistress pregnant than his wife: **2 TIMES**

Number of women who say emotional infidelity is worse than sexual: **3 IN 4**

Buy a Spy

Should you ever need to hire a private detective, do some investigating of your own first. In most states, private detectives must log 6,000 hours in the field, pass a rigorous background check, and possess at least $1 million in liability insurance to be licensed. Go to tracersinfo.com/links/pi_licensing.html to check credentials.

Next, call the dick's office at an odd hour. A reputable private eye will offer 24-hour service, says Sergio Serritella, a licensed private detective in Illinois and owner of Tactical Solutions Group. "A husband who just got info on where his cheating wife may be will want immediate action," he says.

Everything check out? Ask about rates. The industry average is $55 per hour for physical surveillance and $75 per hour for general investigative work, such as tracing a license plate. Top-notch private detectives could charge up to $150 an hour, but so could impostors.

Escape the Web

How does a guy stay faithful when high-speed DSL gives new meaning to the term "quickie"? "Because there's no physical contact, online affairs are very easy to see as separate from one's 'real' life," says Beatriz Mileham, PhD, author of a recent study that found that 83 percent of married men involved in online affairs didn't consider it to be cheating—though 0 percent would tell their wives. If you're having an e-fling and count yourself among the 17 percent of guilt-ridden guys, cut out all instant messaging, e-mailing, and Webcam canoodling. Give willpower a week or two. If, at the end of that time, you still haven't broken things off, fess up to the missus. Then regain her trust with a spyware program like eBlaster ($150), which sends copies of all online correspondence to the administrator, aka your wife. It's a double deterrent: Not only will you rat yourself out in real time, but you'll also hand her evidence for the divorce suit.

Number of unavailable men who go online and say "I'm available": **1 IN 5**

Number of women who do the same: **1 IN 10**

Number of divorce suits sparked by online affairs: **1 IN 3**

Percentage of men who'd pay $10,000 to keep someone from exposing their infidelity: **4**

Amount the average adulterer drops on his lover annually: **$12,000**

Percentage of couples who manage to stay together after an affair: **70**

Percentage of unfaithful women who cite "loneliness" as the reason they had an affair: **22**

Percentage of philandering men who say they "only needed the perfect opportunity" to cheat: **22**

Top reason a man won't leave a perfidious partner: **HER YOUTH AND ATTRACTIVENESS**

Top reason a woman won't walk out: **HIS INCOME AND STATUS**

Number of two-timing guys who say that, in the end, cheating wasn't worth all the trouble: **1 IN 4**

Celebrity the average guy would most like to have an affair with—even if he was certain to be caught: **HALLE BERRY**

Second place: **SALMA HAYEK**

The Disposable Male?

BY DAVID ZINCZENKO

I T SENT A CHILL THROUGH ME, and when I recounted it to other men on staff, they squinched and shivered the same way.

Our features editor Jeremy Gerard, mentioned a phenomenon he'd witnessed sweeping through his friends and neighbors. "Every couple I know seems to be getting divorced," he said. "And the women are instigating it." Repeatedly, Gerard said, he and his wife heard the same thing from their women friends: "I have a career, I have financial independence, and I'm tired of putting up with him."

Now, I'm the first one to admit that a relationship's chances of survival rest in no small part on a woman's willingness to put up with the man in her life. Men are a lot better at shutting out the unpleasant white noise of their mates. Women, on the other hand, are more finely attuned to the rhythms of life and of love and understand that sometimes gentle hints and reminders ("Hey, it's October 21. Didn't someone we know get married on that date?") help to goose men along in fulfilling their husbandly duties. Women don't shut out the white noise. And maybe they're getting tired of listening.

As Nicole Beland, the *Men's Health* Girl Next Door columnist, points out, young women today don't expect a man to take care of them. "Their priorities are an education, a career, and a financial strategy," Beland explains. "And a man, if he happens to come along, would be a nice addition."

By 2013, female college grads will outnumber men getting degrees by three to two. That means for every entry-level job, we'll be outnumbered by women who are just as hungry as we are to get their feet in the door.

Is this a crisis for men? No, but it does mean we need to find a new way to measure our suitability for the opposite sex. Traditional male roles aren't shifting—they've shifted. And if it's not stability, a home, and the comfort of a warm paycheck that women want from us, what do we have to offer?

A lot, says Beland. But it's time to take stock of where we are and to reset the course for where we're headed. (See "Babes in Boyland" on page 50.)

Sounds of Seduction

BY JESSE KORNBLUTH

WHEN IT COMES TO BEDROOM MUSIC, it's time to get over Barry White. No lady's impressed by these stale seduction songs. "Can't Get Enough of Your Love, Babe"? Please. The guy's dead—and clichéd. Let him rest in peace.

Bryan Ferry is very much alive, however, and *Boys and Girls*, a solo effort from 1985, will reward you for a thousand and one nights. The drums and bass lay down a groove so deep it might as well be carved; the guitars are eloquent, the backup singers celestial. And then, in the lyrics, Ferry pours on romantic desperation.

But the words are just mantras, as Ferry—an English coal miner's son who grew up to lead Roxy Music—is more obsessed with suaveness and drama than with proving a point. It's the perfect background music for making your move.

There are times when it's better to play music with no lyrics—or none you understand. For those nights, I'm a big fan of rai, the addictive pop music from Algeria. Khaled is considered the king of rai, and he proves it on *Sahra*, a CD that artfully blends Middle Eastern sounds and a reggae beat. Or I look to Brazil, where Virginia Rodrigues creates some of the moodiest, dreamiest music I've ever heard. Everything she's recorded is first-rate, but start with *Nos*, Portuguese for "Us." Light a candle. Press "play." In the morning, she'll thank you.

The Moody Clues

She doesn't expect you to understand all of her emotions.
But our five simple tips will keep her happy—and you satisfied.
Read on for some advice

BY KATE DAILEY AND ERIN HOBDAY

THERE'S NO EASY WAY to explain how a conversation with a woman can go from sexy to sour in seconds. Maybe she had a bad day at work or didn't get enough sleep. Or maybe you left the seat up. Sometimes the old "hormones" excuse is the cause; they affect neurotransmitters in her brain, says Donnica Moore, MD, founder of DrDonnica.com. Here's a navigational tool for the peaks and valleys of a woman's feelings.

FORGET YOURSELF. "Men often assume that a woman's moodiness is about them and get angry—that's usually the worst thing that can happen," says Joshua Coleman, PhD, author of *The Lazy Husband*. Consider what else may have gone wrong in her day. Showing that you think about her will go a long way toward improving the situation.

AVOID THE "P" WORD. If she happens to be PMS-ing, don't suggest it's the cause. Just go along with whatever's ticked her off—she's right, it's unforgivable that Rite Aid ran out of Mint Milanos.

SEEK THE NAKED TRUTH. Women want sex to be part of the psychic glue of the relationship, but they can be timid about asking for what they want in bed. If she feels you haven't picked up on her hints, she's going to think you aren't connected.

INVESTIGATE, BUT DON'T GET DEFENSIVE. Many men interpret feedback as criticism, says Coleman. Shutting down to her suggestions makes her feel shut out—and no one wins.

GET EVEN. An uneven division of labor often sets off her moods, says Cathi Hanauer, editor of *The Bitch in the House.* "Women are obsessed with things being equal, largely because they generally end up doing more," Hanauer says. Tackle one of her regular tasks: Cook dinner, walk the dog, or make a run to the grocery store.

BE KING KONG. "When a woman's bitchy, she often wants to be Fay Wray and yell and beat her fists on your hairy chest," says Regena Thomashauer, author of *Mama Gena's Marriage Manual.* Your job: Let her vent, without bitching back. And don't feel as if you have to fix what's irking her. Instead, draw her a bath, brush her hair, rub her back. She'll remember—and repay you—when she's in a better mood.

Don't Get Dumped

She left you on the curb. She said, "It's not you, it's me." Here's the
truth—and why this will never happen to you again

BY CHRIS CONNOLLY

I**T'S THE ONE-SIDED REJECTION** and door-slam finality that bites.
Things seem to be going swimmingly until she hits you with "Look, I
like your hustle, but I just don't feel it anymore." Which, processed by
the male brain, registers as "Get lost, loser." And you're left standing
alone in the rain. The worst part? Most of the time, you don't even
know why. You just know it hurts.

We surveyed more than 5,000 women in a MensHealth.com and
Glamour magazine Web poll to find out why women dump men and
what's going on in those vicious heads when they do. For starters, ignore her "It's not you, it's me" cliché.

"Actually, it's you," said 40 percent. Only 4.8 percent said, "It's
me." The rest said, "It's a little of both."

"Women don't enjoy ending their relationships," says Logan Levkoff, a PhD candidate and New York City–based sexologist. "It's not
a decision they make lightly." So why do they? Here's the rundown.

If you're always fighting with each other and the thrill is gone,
be happy she beat you to the trigger. And if you're cheating, you de-
serve it, man. You can assume that's automatic grounds for dumping.
Heck, 18 percent of women said they'd pull the plug even if you just
kissed another woman, and 9 percent put chronic flirting on the must-
dump-him list. So focus your charm on her, not the one over there.

"Cheating usually results in a dump by default because you're never given the chance to have The Talk," says Kristina Grish, 28, author of *We Need to Talk. But First, Do You Like My Shoes? Dress Codes for Dumping Your Man.*

Other than that, if you don't want to get dumped, there are ways you can avoid it.

REASONS WOMEN GAVE FOR BREAKING UP

Too many arguments and conflicts: **26 PERCENT**
No chemistry: **18 PERCENT**
Found a better guy: **14 PERCENT**
He cheated: **11 PERCENT**
He wouldn't commit: **11 PERCENT**
He wasn't husband material: **9 PERCENT**
I wouldn't commit: **8 PERCENT**
Lousy sex: **3 PERCENT**

Sixty-one percent said a man's potential as a husband and father was "extremely important," and 33 percent thought it was at least somewhat important. "I broke it off with a man I was head over heels in love with because he just couldn't seem to get his life in order," says Nicole Beland, 30, the *Men's Health* Girl Next Door columnist. "Everything about him screamed bachelor: the dirty futon that served as his couch, the extremely low balance in his bank account, the fact that he was still going out 5 nights a week. He didn't do the things a man would have to do to show he could be a good husband: calling me to make sure I got home safely when I was driving late at night, including me in his future plans, pampering me a little when I was feeling sick. Things like that. And he was 32."

Don't let this freak you out, however. "A lot of the qualities that create attraction in women are the same things that would make a man a good father: affection, trust, and communication skills," says Ian Kerner, PhD, a clinical sexologist and the author of *She Comes First.* "When guys think women are evaluating them as husbands and fa-

The Hard Truth: What Women Said about Ending It

How long do you typically think about dumping a man before you actually do it?

Days: 23 percent

Weeks: 54 percent

Months: 23 percent

Last time you dumped a man, how did you tell him it was over?

Telephone: 22 percent

Face-to-face in private: 55 percent

Face-to-face in public: 6 percent

E-mail or letter: 5 percent

Just stopped taking his calls: 11 percent

How long did it take for him to realize it was really over?

Immediately: 25 percent

Several days: 25 percent

Several weeks: 24 percent

Several months: 18 percent

Someone still calls and hangs up, and it's been 2 years now: 6 percent

Who has influence on whether you'll dump a guy?

Girlfriends: 25 percent

Guy friend: 4 percent

thers, they're missing the point. It's really about quality of character."

Seventy-six percent of women have considered dumping a guy in the first 4 months. Women know very quickly. "I've never gone on a third date with a guy I didn't end up staying with for 2 years or more," says Beland.

Family: 16 percent

No one: 55 percent

When you break up with someone, the reasons you give are . . .

True and complete: 29 percent

Truthful, but not the whole story: 50 percent

Vague half-truths so he doesn't feel too bad: 18 percent

Lies: 2 percent

When you say "I hope we can still be friends," do you mean it?

Yes: 64 percent

No: 36 percent

Are you actually still friends with a guy you dumped?

Yes: 60 percent

No: 40 percent

What are the chances you'll hook up casually in the future with a man you dumped?

Very good: 14 percent

He might get lucky if I'm drunk or lonely: 48 percent

No chance: 38 percent

Source: Web survey of more than 5,000 women by MensHealth.com and *Glamour* magazine

Then they give it a few months before reevaluating. "At the 4-month mark in every new relationship, I start to think about whether I want to continue dating a guy or break up with him," says Grish. "They're unconscious inclinations, but by then we've spent enough time together that I can't help but listen for the L-word or look for

The Indispensable Man

The informal part of our survey was conclusive: A man who's great at oral sex is a man a woman wants to keep around. "Forget everything you've seen in porn flicks," says clinical sexologist Ian Kerner, PhD. "When you go down on a woman, make your first lick a slow and tender, full 'ice-cream' lick—start at the base of her vaginal entrance, the fourchette, and work your way up to the top. As you go over the clitoral head, brush it lightly as if your tongue were a feather. Don't think of oral sex as foreplay; think of it as core-play: a complete act of lovemaking that can lead her through the process of arousal to orgasm." A few master strokes:

Horizontal Motion: Most tongue strokes are vertical. Brisk horizontal licks back and forth across the clitoral head will inflame her.

Cat Licks: Work the entire vulva with short, repetitious licks. Save the clitoral head for last, then apply more focus and pressure.

Shadow Finger: Let your index finger trail behind your tongue. The finger's hardness will create a pleasing contrast after your soft tongue. Start with simple vertical and horizontal strokes, then try more complex paths.

Flat Tongue, Still Tongue: Let your tongue rest firmly, flat against the full length of her vaginal entrance. Let her move and grind against your tongue.

signs that indicate whether he's with me to have fun or because he actually sees a potential future together."

Around 4 to 6 months is a common transition point. "The early stages of a relationship are very exciting—all your sex chemicals are really firing in the brain," says Kerner. "After that, it becomes more about security and well-being. Some people have a hard time transitioning from the falling-in-love phase to the attachment phase." If you're attached and committed, make sure she knows it. If you love her, tell her—and show her. Talk about the future with her in it. Give her a reason to stay, and she will.

There's always hope, even on D-day: Forty percent of the women surveyed said a man had talked them out of dumping him. "I was mid-dump with a man," says Anne, 24. "I told him I couldn't have a relationship with someone who was so closed off. He didn't say anything. After a few minutes, he started crying and explained that this was a problem he had with women. He said he wanted to try harder to communicate with me. His honesty and openness gave me hope, so I decided to stick around."

Magic words that convince a woman to stay: "I love you" or "I'll change." Sounds too easy, but hey, that's what the survey said. But don't say them if you don't mean them. "Truly take into consideration what she's saying and think about whether you can change these things," says Levkoff. "Sometimes you can; sometimes you can't. But don't sacrifice your own identity or you'll wind up unhappy."

Picture Perfect

The woman in your life looks great naked. Having her pose nude can be a thrill for both of you. Here's how to make it happen

BY JESSE KORNBLUTH

ASKING THE WOMAN you're sleeping with to pose for sexy photos or a video is a matter of trust. "The woman has to trust that the man won't exploit her images on the Internet or show them to all of his buddies," says Michael Castleman, author of *Great Sex*. Let her keep the tape or memory card (or Polaroids, if you're old school). And ease into it.

DON'T RUSH PREPRODUCTION. Most women are not exhibitionists. "This is going to be a personal and emotional stretch for her, so go slowly," says Castleman. "If you see photos that turn you on, show them to her and ask, 'Would you ever consider modeling like that?'" Start out by taking pictures of the parts of her body she likes.

CONSIDER WARDROBE. Don't insist on the full monty right away. "Some of the most beautiful photos are shots in which you're not showing everything," says photographer Scott Nibauer. (Think Marilyn under a sheet.) Put her in one of your button-down shirts or a knee-length slip. "This allows her to choose what she's going to reveal and when she's going to reveal it," says Castleman.

PLAN A SCREEN TEST. Test photos are easily attained—and deleted—with a digital camera. Or plug the video camera into the TV, but don't insert a tape yet. "Once she sees herself on-screen, she might get over the fears," says Maggie Berman, cowriter of *How to Have a XXX Sex Life*.

KNOW THE PLOT. Staging a video is less intimidating if you make it seem like a movie with characters. "Encourage her to live out her fantasies on camera," Berman advises. If she's always wanted to wear a French maid costume, try it now.

ENSURE THAT THERE'LL BE A SEQUEL. "Be prepared that the fantasy you had in mind might not turn out as heavenly as you imagined," says Berman. Whatever the result, play up the positive. "Find something you admire, and let her know." She'll be much more willing to try again.

The Man's Guide Cost of Staying Single

A wedding may seem expensive, but bachelorhood can be too.
Here's what a solo life could cost you every year

BY ERIN HOBDAY

YOU'LL NEED: Regular massages and an ergonomic desk chair

RESEARCH SHOWS: After the wedding, men tend to exercise more. Exercise has been shown to relieve chronic back pain.

IT'LL COST YOU $1,500

YOU'LL NEED: A chunk of your paycheck

RESEARCH SHOWS: Married folks retire with 76 percent more dough than singles do. You'll have to stash more in your 401(k) each month to afford that condo in Boca.

IT'LL COST YOU: $1,000

YOU'LL NEED: Ginkgo biloba and dental work

RESEARCH SHOWS: Singles have a higher incidence of alcohol dependence than coupled people do. Heavy drinking impairs memory and increases the risk of periodontal disease.

IT'LL COST YOU: $262

YOU'LL NEED: Prozac and an hour on the couch

RESEARCH SHOWS: Major depressive episodes occur more frequently among unmarried men.

IT'LL COST YOU: $1,830

YOU'LL NEED: Physical therapy and a night in the ER

RESEARCH SHOWS: Single men are injured in traffic accidents more frequently than married men are.

IT'LL COST YOU: $1,117

YOU'LL NEED: A car-enthusiast club membership and monthly gym fees
RESEARCH SHOWS: Unmarried men are more likely to spend their cash on memberships in hobby and health clubs.
IT'LL COST YOU: $284

YOU'LL NEED: Blood-pressure medication and monitor
RESEARCH SHOWS: High blood pressure is less prevalent among wedded men.
IT'LL COST YOU: $114

TOTAL: $6,107

QUICKIES

MEET THE MRS.

How's this for defeating a purpose: Dating lots of women can hurt your search for The One. When prospects are plentiful, "at the first sign of a problem, men often move on to the next woman, instead of dealing with it," says Susan Campbell, PhD, author of *Truth in Dating*. Do these scenarios sound familiar?

YOU'RE SETTING A BUDGET. "If you go into a date thinking, *How much money am I going to spend?* you're sabotaging yourself," says Bill Horst, of the William Ashley agency, a matchmaking service.

THE FIX: It's fine to go on free or cheap dates. Taking money out of the equation will put the emphasis back on getting to know someone new.

YOU HAVE NO FEMALE FRIENDS. According to Campbell, people often meet through mutual friends. So you need girl friends for dating PR.

THE FIX: If you're not into her, kindly say you just want to be friends. If you impress her with your charm, you might meet her hot roommate.

YOU SCREEN HER CALLS: "If you stop communicating with someone for no clear reason, there's a problem," Campbell says. This is often a prelude to eternal bachelorhood.

THE FIX: Practice dealing with difficult situations, advises Campbell. If a woman says something that turns you off, tell her why it bothered you.

ARE YOU JUST LONELY?

You felt relieved when you broke up with your girlfriend for being too clingy/bossy/psycho/not Charlize Theron. So why do you have doubts now?

It's a mind trick. "Love relationships 'live' in the limbic connections of the brain," says psychiatrist Daniel Amen, MD. "Your brain still looks for her when a memory triggers those emotional connectors." Plus, you miss the sex. Do this.

- Try to remember the last time you had fun with her. If that takes a few moments, don't have second thoughts.
- Look for a pattern in your relationships. Sometimes ambivalence leads a man to let a good woman go because he can't decide if she's The One. If this has happened more than three times, consider professional help to break the cycle.

HEAD TO HEAD: BLONDE VERSUS BRUNETTE

Say you're faced with the unfair dilemma of choosing between a sultry, brown-haired beauty or a gorgeous, flaxen-headed hottie. (The redhead already left with your buddy.) What would you do? To help you out, we compiled the research and consulted some of the brightest minds on the matter.

LOOKS: In a recent survey on the world's most beautiful women by AskMen.com, 10 were blondes, nine were brunettes, and there was one redhead. (Isn't there always?) The reason blondes led the field? "Golden hair brings out the color of the eyes and makes teeth look whiter," says Natalia Ilyin, a psychologist and the author of *Blonde Like Me.*

Advantage: Blonde

FIDELITY: Men typically want brunettes as wives. A test by anthropologist Hans Juergens revealed that personal ads placed by brunettes looking for husbands received twice as many responses as those posted by blondes. "Blondes tend to be bigger risk-takers and are more likely to want to play around," says psychologist Tony Fallone, PhD.

Advantage: Brunette

SUGAR-MAMA POTENTIAL: Research has shown that brunettes have more job security, says Fallone. His research on hair color and psychology also found that men perceive brunettes as more intelligent and reliable, while blondes are considered flaky.

Advantage: Brunette

WINNER: Brunette. See what brown can do for you.

DUO IN DISGUISE

Consider Halloween a way to take your role-playing out of the bedroom, or at least a chance to ditch your boring daytime self for a night. "Subtle is always better," says Diana Khron, of buycostumes.com. "People like to think about the link between two costumes." Some of our favorites:

- The Donald and Omarosa (a toupee for you and head bandage for her)
- The White Stripes (any combination of red and white, with black wigs)
- Kobe and wife (you wear a Lakers jersey, she wears a giant fake-diamond ring)
- Paris Hilton and a guy with a video camera
- Peter Parker and Mary Jane (you in a Spidey shirt under a button-down, her in a red wig and clingy white shirt)
- A plug and socket (buycostumes.com's biggest seller last year)

ASK THE GIRL
NEXT DOOR
The honest truth about women
from our lovely neighbor

Okay to Vacay?
**How soon is too soon to ask a woman you're dating to go away
with you for the weekend?** —B.N., DENVER, CO

Your invitation will seem premature if you haven't already spent at
least one weekend together in your hometown, lounging around in
bed, taking walks, and everything else in-love couples do between
Friday and Sunday nights. If you've already passed that milestone,
she'll more than welcome the idea of doing all the same romantic crap
in a different location.

Girls Gone Velcro
Why are so many women clingy? —K.S., GAINESVILLE, FL

An evolutionary psychologist would tell you that females hold on to
romantic relationships more tightly than males do because women
want reassurance that the man won't split during pregnancy and its
demanding, endless aftermath. (If a guy thinks calling every day is a
drag, what happens when the baby is crying at 3 a.m. for the 20th
night in a row?) But the big difference that I see between my clingy
and nonclingy friends is that the needy ones have yet to develop a
knack for making themselves happy, so they depend too heavily on
the attention of their boyfriends for a sense of fulfillment. The
women I know who appreciate having space to breathe within a relationship usually have a lot of other things going on in their lives—
stuff that provides pleasure and satisfaction. In other words, if a chill
chick is what you want, seek out babes with good friends and serious
hobbies.

6

IN CHECK

In every relationship, there are obstacles. It's these obstacles, however, that help keep everything in check. You may encounter problems here or there that impact your sex life and, hence, your relationship. But there are ways to conquer such difficulties without sacrificing the partnership you've worked so hard to maintain.

Such obstacles can be lost libido (hers or yours), erectile dysfunction, or simply not enough variety. This last chapter covers the various problems that arise from time to time and the solutions, tricks, and techniques you can use to overcome them to make sure you keep everything in your relationship in check.

Four Quick Tricks That'll Restore Her Lost Libido

Regaining control of your erection on/off switch doesn't mean much if her sex button is stuck. Luckily, some of the clichéd moves men have used to get women in the mood still work—but for entirely different reasons

1. Buy Her a Lobster Dinner

Old Theory: Your class and taste impress her; your willingness to pick up the tab leaves her very appreciative.

New theory: Lobsters are a great source of phosphorus, the K-Y Jelly of minerals. "Phosphorus is important to help keep the vaginal tissues lubricated," which will help increase her comfort level and desire, says Pamela Madison, director of the Women's Sexuality Center in Santa Barbara, California. Order a side of carrots—beta-carotene raises blood levels of progesterone, a hormone linked to increased desire, says Madison.

2. Light Candles

Old Theory: Candles equal romance; romance equals sex.

New theory: Picking the right scented candles can reduce her anxiety and put her in a more receptive mood for sex, says Alan Hirsch, MD, director of the Smell and Taste Treatment and Research Foundation in Chicago. Go for the aroma of green apples; tests show it's one of the top scents for reducing stress in women. But avoid cherry. "We found that it inhibited sexual arousal," says Dr. Hirsch.

3. Slip Her a Sex Pill

Old Theory: She unknowingly swallows Spanish fly; minutes later, she wants to do the horizontal mambo.

New Theory: Tell your partner about ArginMax and maybe she'll slip some to herself. In a study published in the *Journal of Sex and Marital Therapy*, women taking this supplement reported almost twice the increase in sex drive experienced by those taking a placebo. The secret may lie in L-arginine, one of the pill's main ingredients. "L-arginine enhances the production of nitric oxide, which relaxes blood vessels and could improve desire," says Cynthia Finley, RD, a nutritionist at Johns Hopkins University Bayview Medical Center.

4. Re-Create a (Hot) Date

Old Theory: Makes you look like a sensitive, thoughtful guy.

New Theory: Whether you went to the movies or met for coffee, re-create the smell that dominated the date. "If she was sexually aroused by the scent in the past, reintroducing it will create the same arousal," says Dr. Hirsch. That's because the same part of the brain handles scent and emotions. So if you saw, say, *Jerry Maguire* in the theater, buy the DVD and Orville Redenbacher's Smart Pop Movie Theater microwave popcorn; it has all the aroma with none of the saturated fat.

Sizing Me Up

The penis spammers implied that he lacked length, girth,
and staying power. Ha! He'd show them . . .

BY JOE QUEENAN

LET'S BE HONEST: Many men have astoundingly small
penises. When a man receives spam from a company offering to reduce his debts, improve his credit rating, or restore his hair, he is likely
to perk up and listen. Why, then, do so many men take umbrage when
a similarly helpful company offers to provide much-needed help in
the groinal region?

By and large, the people who send the spam are rock-solid Americans trying to make this a better society by bringing much-needed relief to the tens of millions of Americans who have tiny penises.

How do I know this? Because in the time-honored tradition of
serious journalism, I did my homework.

One day I received an e-mail from a company called New Health
Discoveries, which offered a 5-day course in maximizing penile effec-
tiveness. I immediately signed up, not because I'm unable to operate
my penis, which has been running like a Swiss clock since puberty, but
because a man can never have too much help in this area. I also expressed interest in becoming an "affiliate" of the company, marketing
phallus-oriented products much the way women sell Tupperware.

I fired off an e-mail to a man named Shawn Moore, which read, "My biggest question is technique. I want to sell these products to all the employees at my firm (about 350 men), but how do you bring up the subject of penises without embarrassing them?"

A little while later, I received a very nice message from a man identified as "Ford." "It's a touchy subject. My best suggestion would be to somehow bring it up in conversation. Possibly mention how they have worked for you. You probably have to know a person well enough to know if you can bring up the subject."

Meanwhile, Shawn, my original contact, sent me an e-mail explaining how to go from being a "1-minute man" to "a master in the bedroom." This involved a series of easy-to-do exercises for the pubococcygeus (PC) muscle. Basically, I was instructed to tense it until my penis "jumped," and repeat 24 times daily. All without looking at photographs available elsewhere on the Internet.

I appreciated the penis-coaching tips I received from Shawn but must admit that they lacked the personal touch. Ford, by contrast, was right there in my corner. I barraged him with queries. In one, I noted that I was thinking of giving some of the company's products to customers as gifts "so they know what I think about the size of their penises." I also asked, "If I give you the names of 25 people I know with tiny dicks, can I get a better price on my own supply?"

While I waited for a response, other concerns reared their ugly heads. One of the things men fear most is that information about their penis size could fall into the wrong hands. Seeking solid advice on this matter, I e-mailed Shawn to say, "I hope my name will not appear on any list of Americans with small penises. Sure wouldn't want that to fall into the hands of John Ashcroft!"

Shawn and Ford obviously stay on top of their correspondence, because the very next day I received this message: "People like John Ashcroft and Dick Cheney probably would have a need for a product like this . . . but then again, aren't they big enough dicks already?"

Not all of my interactions were as fruitful as this one. One company failed to respond when I asked, "Did one of my ex-girlfriends give you my name? Someone named Annie? About 5'4", from northern California? That bitch!"

But other companies did spring into action. For example, after reading that a product called Sativol contains enzymes from certain grasses, I phoned the distributor and explained that I was highly allergic to Serengeti dabbled sprocket grass. When I expressed my medical concerns, Mary, the customer-service rep, actually went and got a bottle and checked to see what enzyme it contained. You think you get that level of service from computer companies when your motherboard explodes?

And it wasn't just Mary. In my experience, I found many of the entrepreneurs and service people in the penis-expanding biz to be forthright and cooperative and, in most cases, more than willing to accept input from the general public. For example, the promotional materials for Pro + Pills report that the male-enlargement products contain "some of the same type of herbs found in Polynesia, where the men of the Mangaian tribe have sex on the average of three times a night, every night."

Immediately, I fired off an e-mail to the man who had supposedly developed the product: "If members of the Mangaian tribe have three orgasms a night, how many will they have if they take your pills? I have some Polynesian guys working on my property, and if I could get them tired out at night, they'd stop grabbing my wife's ass during the day."

I waited a reasonable time to see if the company would respond, then called the firm directly. In due course, I hooked up with a guy named Steve Heller and explained that his company might be low-balling the Mangaian tribe with the three-orgasm figure. Steve said, "It would require some research to find where all that information is archived."

Still, it sounded as though if I really pushed him, the data would be mine.

In the end, my most heartening experience occurred when I spoke with "Jack," a sales representative from BigPenisForever.com. I'll be honest with you: Our conversation got off to a rocky start. He was mystified when I explained that I was researching penis-enhancement products for a major national magazine. At one point, when I asked him which profession had the smallest dicks, he shot back: "Journalists."

"Not this one, pal," I responded, trying to hold my temper in check. "I'm packing an armadillo in here. It's a mastodon, a juggernaut, a jackhammer."

Jack laughed and insisted that he was only joking, that this was the sort of thing guys said around the gym. This led to my next question: Did gym employees secretly walk through the showers, taking notes, and then feed penis-extension firms the names and addresses of men with small penises? Was there a registry of underendowed men? And if so, did BigPenisForever.com use such a list?

"No," he said. "We don't have to find men. They find us, just the way you did."

"Well, let me ask you a question, then: Do you use these products? Have you ever used them? Do they work for you?"

Jack did not hesitate to reply. "I am one of the happiest customers of my product right now."

"So that means you needed to have your penis extended."

Jack hesitated. Then he spoke: "Yes."

That kind of settled the credibility issue for me. Jack went on record that he, like millions of other Americans, had come up a bit short in the shorts. So the next time you receive an unsolicited e-mail from a penis spammer and automatically delete it as unwanted slime, maybe you should have a prick of conscience.

These guys make money the hard way.

This Is Only a Testicle

To you, maybe. As for her, let's just say dating can get nutty when you only have one ball

BY MALCOM BEITH

BY THE THIRD DATE, you've covered the basics—family, hometown, college—and it's time to shift the conversation, and the relationship, into more intimate territory. You probably look forward to it. I dread it.

We all have our own tactics. Maybe you innocently bring up the high-school girlfriend who broke your heart—your way of saying, See, I'm sensitive and capable of loving. Or perhaps you opt for a more direct approach and invite her back to your place: See, I'm strong and decisive.

My way is a bit more awkward. In 30 seconds, I reveal a deeply personal reality: "Can I tell you something?" I ask. "Of course," she says. I pause, then: "I had cancer when I was 23. Testicular cancer." Hesitation spreads across her face, and she tilts her head as if to say, "Oh my gosh, I'm so sorry, but no, I'm not really; I'm just at a complete loss as to what to say." Quickly, I continue reassuringly: "It's okay, though—I'm 100 percent fine now. Don't worry. Another glass of wine?"

See, the trick is to transition out with something more lighthearted. Okay, it's not really a trick, per se, in that it (a) tends to happen out of desperation and (b) seldom works. But there's no way to avoid the conversation. I lost a ball 8 years ago and have come to realize that women simply hate to figure this out on their own.

The lump on my left testicle was the size and texture of a pimple. I noticed it as I haphazardly cupped my balls one night. It disappeared a couple of days later, so I forgot about it.

A few months later, pneumonia set in. My doctor asked if anything else had been bothering me. "Well, yeah, my testicle is a little swollen, and I have these back pains," I said. The diagnosis quickly dawned on him: testicular cancer. A full-body checkup and an ultrasound confirmed it. And so, a day before my 23rd birthday, I was wheeled into the operating room for an orchiectomy—that is, they carved out my left nut.

That wasn't the half of it. The cancer had spread to my abdomen and lungs. Doctors gave me a less than 50 percent chance of surviving for 5 years. After 3 months of chemotherapy to shrink the tumors, I underwent retroperitoneal lymphnode dissection, an abdominal surgery that doctors largely consider the most barbaric in the business. After slicing my gut open, the surgeon lifted out my insides and set them on a table while he removed the 4-by-7-centimeter tumor tucked inconveniently between my spinal cord and a major artery. Finally, an explanation for those back pains.

At the time, I was madly in love with Anna. We'd been together for 2 years, and she cared for me throughout the cancer ordeal— shaving my head when the hair started to go, helping me walk after the chemo sapped my strength. Before the chemo, we even visited a sperm bank so I could make a donation. If I didn't survive, she could still have our kids.

Prior to the surgery, we'd been like any other 23-year-old couple: attached at the groin. But whereas the chemo destroyed my sex drive, nursing me back to health turned her on. It took months to get back in sync. And even then, we felt as if we were having sex out of duty, old-person style. Our relationship had prematurely aged. Fifteen months later, she dumped me. It hurt, but it was the right move for both of us. Cancer has a way of taking the youthful exuberance out of things.

Do I miss her? Sure—I wouldn't be alive without her. But what I miss more is not having to explain. With Anna, it was "no ball, no problem."

I'd been given another chance to be young and single. I could flirt, get drunk, and have meaningless flings without telling women anything about me, let alone that I'd survived cancer. After all, one testicle looks like two . . . pretty much.

Eventually, though, my speak-no-evil policy started backfiring. The girl would be feeling around, then suddenly flinch or withdraw. If she was using her mouth, the reaction would be even more pronounced, often accompanied by a "What the . . . ?" Suddenly, I wouldn't feel so turned on. Tears would well up as my erection went down. I'd explain, because I'd have to. But the moment would be gone.

You may be wondering, "Why not get a stand-in?" But 2 years before my surgery, silicone-filled prosthetic testicles were pulled off the market because, like silicone breast implants, they tended to burst and leak into the bloodstream. Saline-filled replacements just received FDA approval in 2002. Besides, my focus has been on survival, not on how I look. If a woman can't live with that, I don't want to know her. That's why I decided 2 years ago that it was in everyone's best interest to come clean before being intimate. The results have been mixed.

Some girls express curiosity: "I've never been with a man with one ball. What does it look like?" Contrary to what you might think, this is not hot at all. Reminds me of too many doctor visits, when a cute young medical student would study my scrotum as if it were finals week. Some girls express fear, which is usually compounded by ignorance. One asked me if testicular cancer is transmittable, like an STD. I laughed; she was dead serious.

Since this talk happens before a single shirt is shed, the woman has no real stake in me yet. Hence, she'll say, "I lost my grandmother to cancer" with a sympathetic look, then offer a hug or a "keep your head up" pat on the back. Harmless enough, but I can almost feel her sexual tachometer retreating from "Right now!" to "Not going to happen."

Perhaps I'm asking too much of the women I date. The truth is, I'm no picnic, either. Two years after treatment, my oncologist gave me the all-clear. "Live your life as if you never had cancer," he said. So I do: I drink like your average twentysomething (even though I'm 30), I eat what tastes good, I work excruciating hours in a job I love, and I don't worry about my body as long as I'm feeling healthy.

I can be a downer, in that I often remind people of their own mortality. One woman I dated briefly a year and half ago asked me about my dreams. "I don't have any," I said. "My dream is to live, and I'm living my dream."

And eccentric? Guilty as charged. You'll find me wandering the streets of New York at 3:30 a.m. It's my favorite time to be alive, because the city feels like it's completely mine. I also sing at the top of my lungs when I'm in a good mood and cry when I hear a beautiful song. I've been known to skip down the street, too.

Normal men don't do that.

Last year, I began seeing a woman who was just spectacular. I was smitten from the start. Not only was she beautiful—just a quick glance into her intelligent brown eyes pretty much had me mesmerized—but she was witty, mature, and above all, thoughtful.

She had a certain toughness, too, and didn't seem like the type who would be scared off by the gory details of my story. I told her about the cancer early on, and she took it in stride. After one particularly alcohol-soaked date, we ended up back at my place. No sex, but that was fine—I was keenly aware that this was the beginning of something big, and I wanted to savor every moment of anticipation.

The only problem: When my sobriety returned, so did all my fears. When the opportunity arose to take a step closer, I'd take a step back. We'd be at a fancy candlelit dinner—me trying desperately to charm the pants off her but terrified of what would happen if I really did. As the sexual tension mounted, so would all my desires—to make her want me no matter what, to sleep with her, to explain all of the things I was afraid of, to not even be in this situation in the first place. Eventually, I'd lose focus, and the evening would limp on to its inevitable conclusion: my lame excuse for calling it a night. A gentle kiss at her door, over, then out.

Before long, she got used to my brushoffs. When she asked why I smoked cigarettes occasionally, I offered up comments like, "Because I can." It was dismissive and disrespectful, but I was just trying to pass myself off as a healthy, carefree young man.

After 3 months, she dumped me. I couldn't blame her. I'd given her every reason to think I was just like every other urban cad she'd dated and dumped: shallow, selfish, inconsiderate, self-destructive.

I knew I'd acted like a jerk, but, frankly, this time, getting dumped was empowering. After 8 years, I finally felt normal again.

Unsafe Sex

Protect yourself

BY KATE DAILEY

A **WILD NIGHT OF SEX** can damage more than your standing with the neighbors. Your health could suffer—and not just from an STD. Here's how to prevent being thrown into pain during the throes of passion.

Broken Penis: Yes, it's as awful as it sounds. When an erect penis is bent at a tight angle, its inner chamber can rupture. Aside from indescribable pain, "you'll hear a crack and have immense swelling and bruising," says Jon Pryor, MD, chairman of urological surgery at the University of Minnesota Medical School. This most commonly happens during vigorous woman-on-top sex. Immobilize your fallen soldier and head to an emergency room; surgery is the only cure.

Back Spasms: If you're already dealing with a temperamental back, sex could be less than enjoyable, warns Donald Hirsh, of the International Chiropractic Association. You're more likely to stay out of traction with her on top. (But take it easy; see "Broken Penis," above.)

Heart Attack: A sex-induced heart attack isn't as common as Anna Nicole might like, but if you're out of shape, any increase in physical activity can be risky, explains Ben Wedro, MD, a doctor of emergency medicine at the Gunderson Clinic in La Crosse, Wisconsin. Drugs like Cialis, Levitra, and Viagra, or other stimulants—legal or otherwise—can also stress your heart. "They all put you at risk of spasms of the coronary artery, which can cause a heart attack," he says. If you're overweight or have high blood pressure or cholesterol, pop an aspirin before bed for added protection.

Latex Allergy: The same people who have banana, avocado, chestnut, kiwi, and tomato allergies likely have latex sensitivity. A full-blown allergy attack—wheezing and hives—demands medical attention. For itchy skin, use over-the-counter antihistamine pills and creams like Benadryl, says Dr. Wedro.

Good Morning, Gorgeous

She's awake, you're awake. What's next?
The encore seduction

BY JENNIFER WORICK

YOU'VE GOT A WOMAN IN YOUR BED. Good work, lad. But is she there in the morning? "Chances are, if a woman hasn't tiptoed out in the middle of the night, she's looking for more than a one-night stand," says Yvonne K. Fulbright, author of *The Hot Guide to Safer Sex*. If you want to ensure repeat visits, treat her well at this point. She's vulnerable and doesn't want to seem trampy, Fulbright says. Know what to expect and what to do (and not do).

DON'T STIFF HER. "A guy who wakes up with an erection is having a physical reaction that I had nothing to do with," says Jane, 34. Your bedmate may not be as ready as you are. "Women usually don't wake up aroused," says Ian Kerner, PhD, author of *She Comes First*. "Cuddle, or whisper in her ear about a sexy dream you had." She can be convinced.

CLEAN UP. She'll want to freshen up. Offer her a spare toothbrush. Or arrive bedside with bagels and coffee, Fulbright suggests. Your friend won't forget the sweet gesture, and it'll ease bad-breath concerns.

COMPLIMENT HER. She'll be thinking about her smeared mascara and tangled hair. You're going to tell her she looks great. "When I woke up with my boyfriend after we first slept together," says Elaine, 30, "he told me how amazing my skin looked in the sunlight. He scored points for making me feel less self-conscious."

THINK AHEAD. "The most impressive thing a guy can do after we've slept together the first time is ask me out for another date before I leave," says Jenny, 26. "That will erase any worries that you think she's easy," Fulbright says, "and it'll up the odds you'll share sheets again."

SLOW DOWN. Keep things relaxed. "Give her a pair of boxers and a T-shirt to lounge around in," Fulbright advises. Bene, 28, appreciates a guy who shares the newspaper. "Reading the paper over breakfast signals comfort and casualness, not to mention intellect." Remember, you are still technically on a date, so let her know you enjoy her company by not rushing her out the door.

Get a Second Look

Moves to make the best impression

IF YOU WANT TO MAKE a good first impression on that woman over there, you're too late. It's done. "As soon as she lays eyes on someone, she has a first impression," says Frank Bernieri, PhD, a social psychologist at Oregon State University. It's what happens next that counts.

BE READY TO FETCH. An animated person is like a tail-wagging dog. And she'd rather play with an eager pup than with a sleeping hound. "People who are expressive, as opposed to poker-faced, are considered attractive," says Bernieri. "They might gesture or posture or have faces that are easy to read, which makes her more secure in their presence. We know where we stand." Think Will Ferrell, not Colin Farrell.

ASK, DON'T TELL. "We're our own favorite subject," says Hurry Date.com CEO Ken Deckinger, "so if we spend the whole time talking about ourselves, we'll remember it as a great experience." Make her feel good and steer the conversation toward her interests—that's what he advises the men who sign up for his speed-dating service. The longer she talks, the more she likes you. Bonus points for remembering what she said.

GET PHYSICAL. Make eye contact and lean forward. You're interested in what she's saying. Women find an attentive man attractive, Deckinger reports. Getting her attention is as simple as giving her yours—and your body language does that.

BE MYSTERIOUS. "Men tend to hold forth on topics they know a lot about," says Ann Demarais, PhD, coauthor of *First Impressions:*

What You Don't Know About How Others See You. Women call this male-pattern lecturing, and it bores the hell out of them. Resist the urge. Instead, intrigue her with a line like, "Next time, I'll have to show you pictures from my trip to Peru."

PLAY THE NAME GAME. We respond to our name more than to any other word. Hearing her name stimulates the right side of her brain, which means she's paying attention to you. Drop her name into the conversation a couple of times. ("Cindy, tell me more about your gymnastics class.") Use it too much and you'll sound like a used-car salesman. Do it just right and she'll find you irresistibly charming—and you'll be able to sell her on anything.

What's Not to Love?

All the love letters and numbers on our most touchy-feely emotion

**GE AT WHICH** the average guy first gets hit with puppy love: **10**

The target of his crush: **A CLASSMATE**

Length of the infatuation: **6 MONTHS**

Number of men who think about their high-school sweetheart: **1 IN 3**

Number of women still wondering about theirs: **1 IN 3**

Number of times the average guy will fall in love: **5**

Location where he says he feels it every time: **HIS HEART**

Runner-up: **CENTER OF HIS CHEST**

Number of men for whom being in love feels a heck of a lot like being high: **1 IN 4**

Illegal drug that gives the same rush as love: **COCAINE**

How long the love-hit usually lasts: **3 TO 7 YEARS**

Percentage of men who say they've felt literally lovesick: **78**

Hormone that increases in men newly in love: **CORTISOL**

Hormone that slowly drops: **TESTOSTERONE**

Psychological condition most closely related to falling in love: **OBSESSIVE-COMPULSIVE DISORDER**

Country that came up with the bright idea of using "love" to mean "zip, zilch, zero" in tennis: **ENGLAND** (from the mangled *l'oeuf*, which means "the egg" in French)

Top reason the average guy thinks people fall out of love: **THEY WERE NEVER TRULY IN LOVE.**

Percentage of men who say it's because "love has a shelf life": **18**

Percentage of men who, given the chance, would tell Tennyson that they'd rather have never loved at all than loved and lost: **16**

Times in the average guy's life that his love's been unrequited: **1**

Amount of time before the average guy will tell the woman he's dating he loves her: **3 MONTHS**

Number of men who secretly love their platonic girlfriend: **1 IN 3**

Percentage of men who reminisce about "the one who got away": **17**

Number who have keepsakes that remind them of her: **1 IN 2**

Inanimate object the average guy is completely head over heels for: **HIS CAR**

Number of men who'd rather hear "I hate you" than "I love you" on a second date: **2 IN 5**

Percentage of men who won't say "I love you" to their partner when other guys are around: **25**

Percentage of men who've said "I love you" in a brothel: **1**

Only actress to play a naked virgin and a naked Venus: **UMA THURMAN**

Percentage of men who would rather find the love of their life than have 6 months of amazing sex: **92**

Number of men who've been dumped because of their love of sports: **1 IN 9**

Number for whom that means a pair of panties: **1 IN 8**

Lock Her Away

FALLING IN LOVE IS EASY; it's climbing out of the stuff that can be difficult. First step toward sanity: "Visualize a file cabinet in your head and take the bad (and good) memories and put them in a file," says Marc Salem, a world-renowned mentalist who stars in the one-man show *Mind Games*. "The stuff is still there in case you want to torture yourself, but it doesn't have to be out all the time." Shrinks call this strategy compartmentalizing.

Now, step two: Buy a real file cabinet. Take all the tangibles—cards, photos, sex toys—associated with the backstabbing bi---, er, that person, and stow them behind steel. Why not simply trash them? Because, says Salem, trying to deny her existence will only ensure her eternal presence in your psyche.

Objects of Our Affection

IT DOESN'T MATTER if it has four wheels or it's a 4-wood—men, more than women, simply love their stuff. But does this mean our emotional evolution stopped with the invention of the television? Nah. "It's a very natural, normal phenomenon [for men] to attach themselves to inanimate objects that serve a soothing function," says Stanley Teitelbaum, PhD, a clinical psychologist in private practice in New York City. In fact, we've been using this stress-squelching strategy our whole lives, only the toys have changed. "As we get older, we replace earlier, soothing things like stuffed animals with other, advanced objects," Teitelbaum says. So embrace it—the idea, not the ᵈ—and figure out which objects will help ease your adult mind. Juₛ ᵣe caution: Know the difference between a pacifier and a prop for a s. ᵣing self-image; the latter is often something you want to show off ᵗ the other boys on the block.

The Man's Guide Cost of Not Having Enough Sex

IF YOU'RE NOT GETTING SOME ACTION at least twice a week, it can cost you in some surprising ways. Show this to your wife or girlfriend so she knows it's in the interest of your health—and your wallet. Otherwise, going without for 3 months could cost you both.

YOU NEED: A gym membership to compensate for lack of physical activity
    RESEARCH SHOWS: Having sex increases testosterone levels, which helps you gain muscle mass and lose fat.
    YOU PAY: $232

YOU NEED: A couple of sick days
    RESEARCH SHOWS: Men who have intercourse twice a week have 30 percent higher levels of immunoglobulin A, which boosts the immune system.
    YOU PAY: $284

YOU NEED: Pay-per-view porn and a subscription to *Playboy*
    RESEARCH SHOWS: Beggars can't be choosers.
    YOU PAY: $54

YOU NEED: A daily aspirin, glass of wine, and fish-oil tablet for heart health
    RESEARCH SHOWS: Sex two or more times a week cuts a man's risk of heart attack or stroke in half—you'll need to take care of your ticker.
    YOU PAY: $321.86

YOU NEED: A massage a couple of times a month for back pain

   RESEARCH SHOWS: Sex causes the hormone oxytocin to surge to five times the normal level; this releases endorphins, which alleviate pain.

   YOU PAY: $739

YOU NEED: To surprise your wife with a romantic weekend

   RESEARCH SHOWS: Desperate times call for desperate measures. Hotel sex is a given.

   YOU PAY: $1,695.68

YOU NEED: Couples therapy

   RESEARCH SHOWS: Lack of intimacy can lead to marital problems and even divorce.

   YOU PAY: $1,500

   TOTAL: $4,826.54

The Divorce Lawyer from Hell

Warning: Keep this article away from your wife. Read this story about Bob Cohen, then eat it

BY TOM ZOELLNER

Y OU CAN CALL Robert Stephan Cohen a tough Manhattan divorce lawyer, label him a hardball negotiator, or recognize him as the guy you certainly don't want your wife to be calling. Donald Trump found out—not once but twice. But whatever you do, don't phone his office and ask for "the Animal," as a potential client once did.

"Have you tried the Bronx Zoo?" responded Cohen. Reflecting on the call, he says, "This guy wanted me to be his Doberman. People come in [to my office] angry; they want me to be their messenger and to skin the other side alive."

In the dismal kind of law that Cohen practices, the "other side" that gets skinned is you. The instigator is the woman you once pledged to love to the point of death, the girl who once stirred ecstatic thoughts in your mind all night long, the one who had been your confidante and best friend. Until now.

Cohen has earned vaults of money by presiding over the disunifications of some of New York City's most powerful couples. He has done Doberman duty for Mike Bloomberg, Christie Brinkley, James Gandolfini, Marla Maples, Tommy Mottola, and Ivana Trump. Pity those on the other side of the courtroom, because this son of a Brooklyn cabbie plays to win.

"People who meet me say, 'Wow, you seem like such a nice guy for a divorce attorney. I'd love to sit next to you at a dinner party.' Then they see me in court, and they say, 'My God, where did that come from?' I'm very committed to what I do. There's never a phone call that goes unreturned or a theory that goes unexamined. The only thing in life that I'm afraid of is not being successful."

It comes as a surprise, then, to hear Cohen's definition of a "successful" divorce: one that never happens.

After 30 years in the field, acting as pathologist to hundreds of failing marriages, Cohen has reached a point where he tries to do everything in his power to prevent court papers from being filed and encourage husband and wife to reconcile. His current thinking about divorce, in fact, is not too far from what the pope would say about it.

"Divorce has become glamorized in this country, and people think it's okay," says Cohen, who has himself been through two. "But it's really not okay. It's probably the most horrible thing you can go through, other than a long and suffering death. It's the death of a family. And that's only the beginning of what's been destroyed. The house is going to go. You may see your kids only once every other Thanksgiving. Assets you thought were safe are going to disappear. You may even be thrown in jail on bogus abuse charges. Everybody is going to have to start new. It is a predictably negative experience, and nobody goes through it without a tremendous amount of pain. I always want very badly to tell people they should not be going through this."

He even wrote a book that will almost certainly cost him business. *Reconcilable Differences: 7 Essential Tips to Remaining Together from a Top Matrimonial Lawyer* covers all the typical flash points (sex, money, and in-laws) and suggests a new role for the divorce attorney: that of trying to send a client home instead of leading him to court, because once a troubled marriage reaches a stage where attorneys enter the mix, the discussion starts to become surreal. The world divides into two realms: Real World, where your heart is being barbecued; and a parallel paper universe—call it Legal World—where grum-bling about your last vacation is labeled "mental cruelty" and you're forbidden from even talking to your wife.

Cohen successfully talks his clients out of pursuing a divorce only about 10 percent of the time. The rest of the couples wind up filing papers, and that's when the real hell starts.

"You can't turn back," he explains. "The professionals are at each other. Positions harden. It spirals out of control. The process is just so ugly, and it affects everything that's important."

In the long run, he says, there are generally more benefits to staying together than to splitting, even when couples are in seemingly bad marriages. As a matter of pragmatism, it makes sense for you to exhaust all possibilities before calling the executioner. At the very least, Cohen advises, don't think that calling a law office is going to solve your problems. It may make things worse.

"Going to see a lawyer should be at the end of the line, when you have absolutely no other options. We're not that good at putting Humpty Dumpty back together again."

So how can a divorce attorney take a position so contrary to his job description? There is a pragmatic answer for that, too, which is why you want to listen to him off the clock rather than on.

"Nothing I do will ever put a 'Gone Fishin'' sign on my door," he says. "I have more business than I know what to do with."

The Divorce Attorney's Guide to Staying Together

Simple strategies for divorce-proofing your marriage

BY ROBERT STEPHAN COHEN

IF I LEARNED ANYTHING in my 30 years in matrimonial law, it's that divorce is rarely a solution. It's a life-altering and devastating process that should be avoided at all costs. Take my word for it, because I know what I know. And I've learned a great deal about what draws two people together and what pulls them apart. Here are some first steps toward improving your marriage and ensuring that our paths never have reason to cross.

1. Just 30 minutes extra a day with your wife can amount to a world of difference in the quality of your marriage. Take a second to calculate the hours on an average day you spend watching TV, surfing the Web, working out, and talking on the phone. Redistribute a half hour to your wife.

2. Does your wife know what an average day at work is like for you? Try taking her to the office for the day or walking her verbally through your routine. Then be a tourist in her workday.

3. Remember that the point of an argument is to be heard and understood. She craves this. Next time you fight, listen for something you can agree with rather than finding more things to refute.

4. Have any sexual fantasies you've always kept from her? Now is the time to share them. Don't be surprised if the response you hear sounds a lot like, "What took you so long?"

5. When you come home from work, give her a long, deep kiss without expecting sex. Let the kiss speak for itself.

6. Don't think that a trial separation will bring you back together. It almost never does.

7. Infidelity is awful. Divorce can be even worse. If your spouse has cheated on you, don't immediately assume the marriage is over.

8. It's natural to want to be your wife's strongest partisan. But when she's in conflict with her family, it's best not to get too involved. She might not forget the things you say, even if you're trying to defend her.

QUICKIES

DOES SHE LIKE TO WATCH?

In the United States, 43 percent of all marriages end in divorce, and 81 percent of the splits are a direct result of conflicts over watching sports. Okay, we made that last part up. But gender-based sporting disagreements (sounds scientific, right?) do cause strife for even the happiest couples, except perhaps for Nomar and Mia. Follow this advice to turn your woman into a sports fan, at least for 3 hours.

Make the game about her. Tell her she's vital to the event because she's your good-luck charm. Ask her to wear your team's jersey. Explain that watching the game with her is quality time and there's nothing you like better than an afternoon of cuddling with her on the couch while your favorite team's on the tube. Heats up the commercial breaks, too.

Make the game a social event. If you want to have the guys over, invite a few of her friends, too. She'll be off discussing *Average Joe* with her girlfriends before the first pitch, leaving your attention to the screen. Or, why not bring her to the sports bar? It's a win-win. She'll feel included, plus she'll be available to manage the pool.

Make the game interesting. Watch her eyes light up if you tell her you heard that Jason Giambi is dating Tara Reid. And that Tom Brady is dating Tara Reid. And that Mike Krzyzewski is dating Tara Reid. And that Yao Ming is dating Tara Reid. You get the idea: Show her the soap opera and she'll be hooked.

BACHELOR BENEFITS

My girlfriend and I have decided to live together without getting married. What can we do to receive the same benefits as a legally married couple? —RAY F., CHICAGO, IL

Your best strategy is to leave a paper trail. List each other as beneficiaries and emergency contacts on insurance forms. Draft a living will specifying that she can make medical decisions for you, and vice versa. Name each other as beneficiaries in your wills, or else the surviving partner is entitled to nothing when the other dies. An easier option: Get married.

INFECTION AND INFERTILITY

The sexually transmitted infection chlamydia can cause infertility in women. Now, new research shows that chlamydia infection in men is linked to infertility, according to the journal *Human Reproduction.* Couples in which the man tests positive for a current or past case of chlamydia have a 33 percent lower chance of conceiving, say Swedish researchers. Most men never realize they have the disease because they have no symptoms, says study author Jan Olofsson, MD, PhD. Get a urine test for chlamydia before you have sex with a new partner, suggests Dr. Olofsson. The infection can be cured with antibiotics.

HAPPIER EVER AFTER

Realistic expectations lead to happier marriages, according to a study in the *Journal of Personality and Social Psychology.* Researchers interviewed 82 pairs of newlyweds and found that couples with high hopes but low relationship skills became the most disappointed if the marriage didn't live up to expectations. "Expect it to be work, and expect to have disagreements—and realize that's okay," says James McNulty, PhD. He suggests seeing a marital therapist with your fiancée to help identify your relationship's weaknesses and develop strategies for dealing with the trouble spots.

INSTANT SEXPERT

Facts of Life

60 Percentage of cohabitating couples who get married within 10 years of moving in together. In that same time period, **38** percent break up.

EXPRESS SEX

I love quickies. How can I get my wife to feel the same?

—J.K., TAOS, NM

Anticipation, friend. Bring up the topic when you're clothed, during the day, maybe in a phone call or e-mail. Reassure her that the quickie "won't become a replacement for romance or those long nights of passionate sex," says Tara Roth Madden, author of *Romance on the Run*. Then let her simmer. When you finally do get your moment alone? Use a few of those precious minutes stimulating her manually to help her reach orgasm as fast as you will. Most important, says Madden: "Keep it hot, quick, and naughty."

ADDICTED TO LOVE

It's official: New love is like a drug, according to research published in the *Journal of Neurophysiology*. Scientists studied 10 women and seven men who had recently become infatuated with someone. The participants were shown a photo of their new loves while functional MRI images were taken. The area of the brain that became active (the caudate nucleus and the ventral tegmental area) is the same region associated with reward and motivation. It's also the part that fires up when we satisfy hunger or thirst—or a drug craving. So don't worry—obsession, exhilaration, and anxiety are normal. "We're slaves to passion—to a biological imperative—for a brief time," says Lucy Brown, PhD, a professor of neuroscience at Albert Einstein College of Medicine and one of the study authors. "It's an unconscious motivational-reinforcement system that's activated."

THE SCARLETT JOHANNSEN EFFECT

How'd she sound on the phone? It matters. A voice holds clues to a person's body shape and sexual behavior, reports a new study of 149 college students, published in *Evolution and Human Behavior*. Researchers recorded the voices of participants counting from one to 10 (that's hot!) and had members of the opposite sex rate each voice. Voices rated attractive belonged to people who were attractive physically (measured by waist-to-hip and shoulder-to-hip ratios) and who had the most sexual experience. So don't turn a deaf ear to a blind date. "At least have a phone conversation before you commit to a date with someone," says study author Susan Hughes, PhD, an assistant professor of psychology at Vassar College. Researchers couldn't pinpoint what makes a voice attractive, but the raters tended to agree on who sounded sexy.

ASK THE GIRL
NEXT DOOR
The honest truth about women
from our lovely neighbor

Naked Review

How important is it to a woman for the man she's having sex with to have a nice body? —DOUG, VIA E-MAIL

When a woman opens her eyes during sex and sees a man's ripped abs in action, it's definitely hot. Seeing a large, doughy mass jiggling in all directions is decidedly not. But neither experience makes or breaks sex for a woman. When it comes to building a woman's arousal and bringing her to orgasm, it's the finesse with which a man kisses and touches, sucks and thrusts that counts. That said, excess flab will definitely detract from a woman's eagerness to rip off a man's clothes, whether she's a stranger in a bar or his wife of 10 years. And during sex, it's like an occasional spritz of water on her sexual fire: It cools it a bit, which is a bummer, but by no means puts it out.

Your Assets

So many times I have heard women say that a man has a great butt. Question is, what constitutes a great butt? —ALEX,
SAN FRANCISCO, CA

Simple: compact, muscular, and round.

Girl on Girl-on-Girl

I found a *Playboy* under my girlfriend's bed. Is she bisexual?
—RYAN, VIA E-MAIL

I doubt it. Funny thing about straight women and porn: A lot of girls are more turned on by an image of Paris Hilton naked and grabbing her ankles than they are by a shot of Jude Law naked and grabbing his tool. I'm one of these girls, and your main squeeze probably is, too. When it comes to having an in-the-flesh sexual experience, I lust for a man's body. But on the page, there's something about a vacant-eyed babe sucking on her bottom lip that jump-starts my hormones. Jenna Jameson—like bodies are simply what I've been taught to associate with naughty fantasies and solo sex ever since I stumbled across my first *Playboy* at age 13. And women still corner the market on the vulnerable yet randy have-your-way-with-me look.

Give Good Gift

What do women want for Valentine's Day? Give me a game plan, please. —EDWARD, SEATTLE, WA

- If it's your first V Day together and you're in love: 1. Send her flowers at work—something other than clichéd roses. Try calla lilies or bird-of-paradise. 2. Give her a copy of your favorite novel, movie, or book of art or photography, or a mix CD of your favorites along with a recent book, DVD, or CD that—from what she's told you—she might like. 3. Give them to her (wrapped) during the dessert of a romantic dinner you've whipped up at your place.
- If she's a casual girlfriend and you want to keep it that way: Invite her out for a Valentine's Day dinner, but nix the gift.
- If you've been dating for more than a year: Buy her something that could conceivably last forever: a painting by a well-respected local artist, a vintage watch or clock, pearl earrings (with small pearls that dangle below the ear), or a cuff bracelet with an embedded stone—jade or ruby.
- If you're married and have done it all before: Offer to cook her breakfast, then surprise her with heart-shaped blueberry pancakes, pomegranate juice, and coffee in a custom-made

V-Day mug. (You can get one at most photo shops.) As for what to put on the mug: a picture of you that will crack her up.

Um, I Don't Know . . .

Most women have strong opinions about how they want to spend their time, so why do they usually say "I don't know" when I ask what they'd like to do on a date?   —STEVE, BOSTON, MA

You're right, we are sure about what we like and don't like. What we don't know is what *you* like. By leaving it up to you to come up with a plan, we can find out a lot: which restaurants and movies appeal to you; whether you're into live music, or sports, or art; if you prefer trendy crowds or low-key hideouts. We also get a sense of how interested you are in us by how thoughtful that plan turns out to be. If you're tired of being put on the spot all the time, make a deal with her. Say you'll come up with great ideas for this Saturday night if she promises to take the lead next weekend. That way, you'll find out how hard she's willing to work to impress you.

INDEX

Underscored page references indicate boxed text.

A Simple Act
   of Kindness

Also by Winston M. Estes

A Simple Act
of Kindness

A Novel

Winston M. Estes

J. B. LIPPINCOTT COMPANY
Philadelphia/New York

Copyright © 1973 by Winston M. Estes
All rights reserved
First Edition
Printed in the United States of America

U.S. Library of Congress Cataloging in Publication Data

Estes, Winston M   birth date
    A simple act of kindness.

    I. Title.
PZ4.E794Si   [PS3555.S8]   813'.5'4   72–3877
ISBN–0–397–00943–7

For Janet Moore Estes

A Simple Act
of Kindness

❧ 1 ❧

I looked at Amy sitting patiently with Kenny cradled in her arms, and I had never seen her look prettier. I winked at her to reassure her that the waiting didn't bother me.

"They also serve who only stand and wait," I said. "That's me."

She dodged a chubby little hand that reached for her hat. The dangling red tassel had caught his eye. She was too late.

"I don't know why I don't cut off this doodad and just give it to him," she said, holding him away with one hand and pulling at her hat with the other.

I started to laugh, but Skeeter cut me short. He escaped from the pen I had made with my legs and darted across the waiting room.

I went after him and brought him back under one arm. He was almost two and squirmed with the strength of a bobcat. He set up a wail. I clamped a hand over his mouth and sat down again with him in my lap. I locked an arm around him and held him firmly. "Now sit still, or I'm going to throw you out the window," I said.

Amy laughed and then frowned. "I'm real sorry, darling, for you to use a perfectly good Saturday sitting around like this."

"Oh, well—it gives me a chance to see the doctor who gets all our money for telling us there's nothing wrong with our children." I tightened my grip on Skeeter.

She glanced at the door. "He's certainly taking his time. We've never waited this long before."

We lapsed into silence. I stared vacantly across the room, pretending an interest in a baby whose mother seemed to expect it. The man opposite us, about my own age and considerably more bored, was watching us. My eye caught his, and he looked away, embarrassed. Amy dangled a key chain in front of Kenny and fascinated Skeeter instead.

From the streets of downtown Fort Worth below came the honk of a horn, the screech of rubber on concrete and the angry blast of a policeman's whistle. In the distance, a siren shrieked, then faded. The gentle whir of the air conditioning was beginning to mesmerize me.

Suddenly, the sound of a buzzer shot through the stillness. The receptionist leaned forward and addressed the gray intercom on her desk. "Yes, Doctor?"

All heads turned toward her as if on a single pivot. Beyond her desk the door opened, and Carrie Holbrook came out.

I recognized her immediately; I recalled everything about her as though five minutes rather than five years had lapsed since I had seen her.

She looked marvelous, as beautiful as I remembered her. She wore a gray tailored suit, perfectly cut and fitted, and a saucy suggestion of a hat on her silky blond hair. Her tall statuesque figure, her lithe movements and regal poise erased five years as if by magic, and there stood Carrie Holbrook again with the sparkling green eyes, while everybody gaped at her in open admiration. She was holding a small boy by the hand.

Before the door clicked shut behind her, I was on my feet moving toward her with Skeeter under one arm. She smiled at the receptionist and then saw me. Ever so briefly, she hesitated, and a flicker of recognition appeared in her eyes. Her name was on my tongue, but before I could say it she looked away, tugged at the child and swept past me out into the corridor without saying a word. I was too startled to call after her.

I stared at the door. She had appeared and disappeared so swiftly that I doubted my own senses. The receptionist was talking into the intercom. A young woman with a baby was crossing the room. Amy's voice brought me to.

"Who was that?" she asked.

I continued to stare at the door and made no reply.

"Who was it?" she repeated with curiosity and amusement.

"Carrie Holbrook. . . ."

"You don't sound too sure."

"She didn't speak to me."

"Maybe she didn't recognize you."

"She did, though." I sat down again. "She did recognize me. I could tell."

Amy ran a hand under Kenny's pants to see if they were wet. "Carrie Holbrook . . . Holbrook . . . your friend in the war?"

"Ben Holbrook—you remember. From Erskine. He got lost over New Guinea. Carrie's his wife."

"I remember now—but you seldom mention them any more."

"We didn't stay in touch. But even after five years, I still miss Ben. We had lots of plans for after the war."

Skeeter was relaxed and drowsy in my lap. The room had thinned out, and the remaining people had settled down again to wait. Some were watching us as if listening. I lowered my voice.

"She remembers," I said stubbornly. "I was a third member of that household. We were a regular trio. Some people probably thought we were a triangle, but we weren't. We were good friends, that's all."

"It's peculiar that she didn't speak, then, isn't it?"

"Sure is," I said, shaking my head. "The last I heard of her, she was living in a place called Foley—a little ranch town the other side of San Angelo. It's not even on the main highway. I pass the turnoff every week. I used to think about taking an extra hour or two and driving over to see her, but it seems that I was always running late, and I just never got around to it. She was teaching school then, but she probably lives somewhere else by now. That was—let's see—late in 1945, as I remember. Almost four years ago."

"She doesn't look like the small-town type," Amy said.

"She's not. She's not the schoolteacher type, either. At least, I never had a teacher who looked like her."

"All mine were old maids with moustaches," Amy said.

"And baritone voices," I added.

Kenny tried to crawl out of Amy's lap. She pulled him back. Skeeter was asleep now.

"How did you know she lived in Foley?" Amy asked.

"After the war, she sent me some papers to sign. I had witnessed Ben's will and insurance—and I don't know what else. I sent the papers back and wrote her a letter, but she didn't answer. That was the last I knew about her."

"She's certainly attractive," she said. "And the little boy was a darling."

"Little boy?" The scene came sharply back into focus. "They didn't have any children. She must have got married again."

"Probably. People do it all the time."

"I guess they do. After all, it's been a long time. The last time Carrie saw Ben was in 1944—July fourteen, to be exact. We were leaving Indianapolis for San Francisco—the Port of Debarkation."

Amy was dabbing at the front of her dress. "I was listening," she said, glancing up, "but Kenny was drooling on me."

"I was just remembering," I said.

"Maybe her second husband is jealous," she suggested. "And wants to blot out his wife's first marriage and friends. Anyway, maybe the little boy isn't hers. He could be a neighbor's or a relative's."

"I doubt it. Carrie wasn't the baby-sitter type. I can't even imagine her tending her own. She was never the motherly type, either."

"Many women aren't until they have children of their own."

I grinned at her. We lapsed into silence and awaited our turn with the doctor. While we waited, I thought about the Holbrooks. Solemn, staid, straitlaced Ben and happy, carefree, gregarious Carrie came back at me larger than life. On the face of it, theirs had been an unlikely match, and I wondered briefly if she had married someone who reminded her of Ben. Then our turn with the doctor came.

❦ 2 ❦

The next week was a busy one for me, and I did not dwell on Carrie Holbrook and her peculiar behavior. From Monday through Friday each week, I stayed on the road for American Business Machines, and in that particular week one of my largest dealers, this one in Abilene, was threatening to change his account to a rival company. I was confident that I could prevent his defection, but Mr. Marsh, our vice president in charge of sales, apparently thought I couldn't do it without his personal assistance. He telephoned me three times during the week to tell me what to do and when to do it.

It would have been easy not to like Mr. Marsh, but the fact remained that I did. I also respected him immensely. He was a fine man. Rather small, he had a bald head fringed with white, a soft, cultivated voice and a benign way of looking through his rimless spectacles that made people think they were close to him personally—until they realized that his mind was on American Business Machines to the exclusion of everything else. I don't think I ever heard him mention his own family or even the weather. It was nothing new to have him make a nuisance of himself with his advice and guidance. Naturally I could not ignore him, but he did play havoc with my schedule. As I drove through the West Texas countryside, my mind worked busily from one town to the next, calculating and refiguring how to meet all my appointments and still get home by Friday night.

I had blanketed West Texas with American Business Machines. After the war, dealers had been standing in line waiting for the manufacturers to retool, an eager and ready market for anything mechanical that came off the assembly line. My job had long since settled itself into a routine of keeping the dealers happy with new and improved models of typewriters, adding machines, calculators and whatever else the designers and engineers could devise and produce. My work had become so predictable that between Fort Worth and El Paso I stayed in the same hotels, ate my meals at the same restaurants and bought gas at the same service stations. I even had a standing reservation on the air flight from Midland to El Paso on Wednesdays and return on Thursdays. My work was pleasant, and it was satisfying. Perhaps I had made it too much my own personal possession and achievement, for on this trip, by the time I had reached San Angelo, I had begun to resent Mr. Marsh's guidance as outright interference.

And yet, as fully occupied as my mind was that week, I could not dismiss Carrie Holbrook's behavior altogether. She would not stay out of sight. She passed before me unbidden at odd and illogical moments; while waiting for a traffic light to change, over a cup of coffee with a customer, on a hotel elevator, crossing a street or tying my shoe, I saw her. With Ben no longer the link between us, perhaps I had become one of the memories that she had filed away to forget. Maybe she had designed a life for herself with no room in it for the past. At the same time, it seemed that she could have spoken to me for old time's sake if nothing else. Surely that would have posed no threat to her new way of living, whatever it was.

But for all that, I suppose that in time I would have put her out of my mind again, perhaps permanently, had it not been for the detour that actually led me through Foley.

Almost a month after that glimpse of her, I had spent the night in San Angelo, and my first appointment was in Fort

(15)

Stockton, 180 miles to the southwest. I had a second in Midland, another 90 miles north and back to the east. It was a frustrating itinerary, for my account in Fort Stockton was a small one, worth the trouble and expense of the drive only as a means to keep out the competition.

As you go west in Texas, the state gets bigger. Trim farms and fenced pastures yield to flattened, thirsty land that lies vast, hostile and shadowless in the hot Texas sun. Scrub oak gives way to mesquite, and grain fields to prickly pear and quivering sheets of prairie grass. Distances, sizes and shapes are deceptive, and what appears to be a hill rising out of the shin oak and sagebrush turns out to be merely an outcropping of limestone, and not a large one at that. A steep rise in the ground ahead proves to be so gentle that you don't realize you have reached its summit until you have gone beyond and trained your eyes on another. The gaunt skeleton of a windmill sits atop the earth like a colossus. A solitary house without features or detail blackens a scrap of sky miles away. This is sun country, where you can chase a heat mirage for mile after mile over land as flat as a tabletop to find, with no warning, the jagged gash of a ravine or a rocky canyon, and the earth taking up again on the other side as though the fracture had existed only in your mind. The sky is so big and so broad that, if you study it for a while, you might get a glimmer of what infinity is all about. The area is sparsely populated, and the countryside is relieved only by endless stretches of barbed wire that fences in nothing and wavering columns of telephone poles that go nowhere.

As San Angelo dropped over the horizon behind me and my rearview mirror reflected the same empty nothingness that lay ahead, I settled down for the dreary trip to Fort Stockton. An hour of steady, relentless driving brought me to a dilapidated filling station that stood guard over a side road from the left, and a pointed marker that read FOLEY—9 MILES. A barricade across the highway and a sign reading DETOUR, CLOSED FOR REPAIRS brought me to a halt. I studied the side road with misgivings. A narrow strip of asphalt winding out of sight, it was as uninviting as the terrain it bisected.

The October sun was high. I looked at my watch anxiously, shifted gears, turned left and set out on the asphalt road to Foley.

The road seemed to have been poured onto the flat earth without foundation or design. The edges were ragged as sawteeth, and the holes, eroded by weather and worn by age, had been left untended. As I bounced along, the vastness of the land before me, behind me and on all sides closed in and caught me up in a strange moodiness. A jackrabbit darted from behind a bush, the only sign of life I had seen since leaving the highway. If there were people at the end of the road, I could not visualize Carrie Holbrook ever having been among them.

I wondered whom she had married and if she had stayed in Foley after all. But surely not—not Carrie, with the beautiful dresses and outlandish hairdos; the first one on the dance floor when the orchestra struck up a lively tune.

"Come dance with me, Pete," she used to say. "This one's too fast for old slowpoke Ben."

Then she would wrinkle her nose affectionately at her husband, and we would go out onto the dance floor, leaving Ben at the table to look on with pride. Carrie was one of those people who had to dance. Something inside her would not be still. She danced as naturally as she breathed. She was weightless, in absolute harmony with the music. When I danced with her, I fancied I danced as well as she did. It was an illusion, but Carrie herself was something of an illusion. She had never been quite real to me, and I liked her that way.

Foley arose ahead of me, shimmering in the morning sun, fragile and tentative, ready to be swooped up by the wind and scattered with the dust. As I drew nearer, the buildings began to separate into the low, nondescript boxes I expected to see. They were dominated by a spidery water tower and a two-story structure that probably was a courthouse, maybe a church or a school.

The road curved into town past a scattering of squalid shacks,

(17)

chicken coops and outbuildings flung at random across the dry earth. The town proper was scarcely more than a tick-tack-toe arrangement of a few wide, treeless streets and irregularly spaced frame houses.

Abruptly, I found myself between two clumps of low, red-brick buildings, separated by a street wide enough to have been a plaza. This was the business district: a grocery store, a bank, a post office, a drugstore, a café, a drygoods store, a barber shop, and one or two unidentifiable establishments. A pickup truck and several automobiles sat at haphazard angles in the middle of the street, but no people were visible. A silence hung over the place. It was a silence of too much time suspended in too large an area, of too little to do and too much space to do it in. The wind blew steadily and with determination.

I drove the short block past Foley's businesses, made a U-turn and drove back. Without plan or forethought, I parked in front of the drugstore and went inside. I was already through the screen door and surveying the dim cluttered interior before it came to me that I had no idea why I was there. A stooped, gray-ing man of perhaps sixty was alone in the rear of the store. I climbed onto a stool at the soda fountain and waited for him to make his way to the front. He came up behind the soda fountain and faced me expectantly but with no apparent enthusiasm. He did not speak.

"Good morning!" I said. "What's the reason for the detour? The sign said repairs of some kind."

"You might say that," he said. "A big truck crashed through a bridge about four miles on down the road. The only way they could detour the traffic around it was to build another bridge. Instead of that, they detoured everybody through Foley. What'll you have?"

"Coffee, I guess—black."

"You'll have to go to the café if you want coffee. Two doors down."

"A Coke will be fine, then."

While he busied himself with the ice and a glass, I wheeled

around on the stool and took in the store. I remembered such a store from my childhood. The ceiling-high, glassed-fronted cases along the walls, the round white-enameled ice-cream tables and chairs with curved wire legs, the wrapping counter with its surface too cluttered to be of much use, the door at the rear through which I could see row upon row of prescription bottles lighted by an unshaded bulb, the sickly-sweet smell of drugs, cosmetics and ice cream filled me with a kind of nostalgia. I was surprised that such places still existed.

"How far is it back to the highway?" I asked.

"Which way you going?"

"To Fort Stockton."

"Not much further. Three miles is about all. Just follow the road you came in on."

He straightened up, placed the Coke in front of me and leaned forward, resting both hands on the back edge of the fountain.

"This your first time in Foley?"

"Yes, it is. I go from San Angelo to Fort Stockton and Midland every week, but this is the first time I ever took the Foley turnoff."

"I reckon you might say we're enjoying a boom," he said with a chuckle. "That detour has sent more traffic through here during the last week than we've had in twenty years put together. Nobody comes here much unless it's on business or unless they know somebody."

"I used to know somebody here," I said.

"That right? Then I reckon I know 'em, too." He warmed to my presence. "What's their name?"

"I don't know what it is now, but it used to be Holbrook. She taught—"

"You mean Carrie Holbrook?" The man's eyes brightened, and his face softened into a wide smile. "Is that who you mean?"

"Why, yes—I guess it is, but I didn't expect—"

"Carrie Holbrook," he repeated. "She's a widow lady. Her husband got killed in the war."

(19)

"That's her," I said quickly. "You seem to remember her well."

"Remember her?" He peered at me curiously. "Remembering doesn't have anything to do with it. She lives right here in Foley right now."

"But you called her *Holbrook*."

"Well—so did you. That's her name. Wasn't that who you asked about?"

"Yes, but—why does—I mean what does she—"

He beamed. "She's a schoolteacher. All the kids think a lot of her. How did you know her?"

"I knew her husband during the war. We were overseas together."

"I bet she'd be glad to see you then," he said. "You can't catch her until noon, though." He glanced at the clock on the rear wall. "If you want to wait around until dinnertime, school lets out at twelve."

I'm not certain how much I was tempted, for now that I had stirred the memory of that brief encounter in Fort Worth, I discovered that it still smarted. I wanted to hear an explanation from Carrie's own lips, but in some perverse fashion, I was reluctant to give her the opportunity. Anyway, I had those appointments in Fort Stockton and Midland.

"Did Carrie—Mrs. Holbrook—didn't she get married again?"

"Not that I know of," the man said.

"Does she live alone?"

"Just her and the boy."

"The boy?"

"Ben—her son. He was born while his daddy was overseas—after he got killed, I think. His daddy never saw him. I know that much." Shaking his head sadly, he said, "He's a cute little fellow."

"How old is—Ben?"

He made some silent calculations. "Must be four years old, maybe five. I don't know for sure. He's not old enough to go